Rachel the 'write' to speak

Sandra Capelin

Rachel the 'write' to speak

Copyright: Sandra Capelin

1st Publication 1992 by Penwell Print, Cornwall

2nd Publication 1997 by Minerva Press, London

3rd edition 2019 by Kindle Direct Publishing, Amazon

Acknowledgements

I would firstly like to thank Marquita Stables and Linda Lascelles for their support and encouragement in making me realise that a 3rd edition of this book was still so vitally needed. I would also like to thank Phil for his assistance with photographs, Rachel for emergency help with IT and Bethany Michael for helping with the cover design. However, I am indebted to Ian Bleakley for not only proof reading the book itself but for all his invaluable patience, help and support.

Please note:
Some names in this book have been altered to protect their identity.

Photographs

Front cover: Rachel aged 4 years

Back cover: Rachel and her daughters

Contents

Forward

It is an honour to write the foreword for Sandra Capelin's biography of her daughter Rachel's long journey to a diagnosis of language disorder. Children with this condition still continue to puzzle and perplex professionals as well as parents. The account of problems encountered by Sandra in seeking recognition of her daughter's difficulties are as vivid and fresh today as they were 30 years ago. We still see many children whose language difficulties are hidden beneath behavioural disturbances that distract from the underlying problem and lead them to be dismissed as wilful or unintelligent. The problem can be compounded when, as in this case, poor understanding of language is disguised because the child can speak in sentences.

It is particularly sobering to read of the teachers who dismissed Sandra's concerns as those of an overambitious parent, reluctant to accept that her child was not a high-flyer. And galling to hear that when, after her mother had worked carefully with Rachel to ensure that she could manage tasks such as writing between lines, her concerns were then dismissed because Rachel's difficulties were not severe enough.

In the course of my own research career, I've seen huge changes in our understanding of children's language disorders. We now know that these can take many and varied forms. For some children, there are evident difficulties with production of sequences of speech sounds. These can have a serious effect on communication, but they are at least obvious and so the child is likely to be referred for speech and language therapy. Other children, like Rachel, have big problems in finding the right words, and become frustrated at inability to say what they mean. All too often these expressive difficulties co-exist with poor language comprehension, but that is hard to recognise unless appropriate tests are done to check whether a child is actually responding to what is said, rather than guessing meaning from the context combined with a limited grasp of two or three words. It's hard to imagine what it must be like going through life with such problems: I suspect the closest many of us can get to understanding it is to imagine ourselves stranded in a foreign city with just a limited spoken vocabulary. You might unfamiliar vocabulary, you could find yourself totally at sea. And as if that was not stressful enough, you may then be scolded or mocked for not doing what was expected.

I'm optimistic enough to hope that publication of this book will help ensure that future generations of children will have their difficulties recognised sooner than was the case for Rachel, who was only diagnosed with a language disorder at the age of 16 years. For us to progress, teachers and other professionals who work with children need to take on board three key points.

First, listen to parents and take their concerns seriously. If a parent senses something is wrong, they are usually picking up on a genuine issue – and the worst thing you can do is to criticise the parent for making a fuss about nothing.

Second, be aware that behaviour difficulties are often the surface manifestation of underlying language problems. Back in 1989, a remarkable study led by Nancy Cohen in Canada considered language functions in a group of children who had been referred to a child psychiatry department. The researchers found that just over half the children had language problems of clinical significance, and in around half of those cases, the problem had never been identified. Since that study was conducted, many others have been carried out in other parts of the world, and the conclusion is clear: we should evaluate language skills of children presenting with behaviour problems, because very often there is a language disorder at the root of their difficulties (see Cohen, 1996, for a review).

A third point is that a language disorder does not always present as difficulty talking. Yes, there are children who find it difficult to string words together in sentences, or who speak unclearly or with evident word-finding problems. But some children learn to chatter away in a superficial way that can mask major problems in understanding. A proper evaluation of receptive language is vital for any child where language concerns have been raised: this can reveal that language disorder is like an iceberg: a large chunk of comprehension failure may lurk underneath the visible expressive difficulties.

Despite the long battle that Sandra had to identify Rachel's problems, the book is ultimately inspiring and encouraging. Sandra illustrates the importance of not only helping your child overcome obstacles, but also identifying things your child likes to do and can succeed in: Rachel loved to dance, and this provided her a means to enjoy herself, socialise and develop self-esteem. Her life became easier once the problems were recognised, but her story demonstrates the importance of finding the right niche, and shows that a language disorder need not be an obstacle to an independent and fulfilling life.

Dorothy V M Bishop FRS FBA FMedSci

British psychologist specialising in developmental disorders specifically, developmental language impairments. St John's Oxford

Reference: Cohen, N. J. (1996). Unsuspected language impairments in psychiatrically disturbed children: developmental issues and associated conditions. In J. H. Beitchman, N. J. Cohen, M. M. Konstantareas, & R. Tannock (Eds.), *Language, Learning, and Behavior Disorders* (pp. 105-127) Cambridge: Cambridge University Press.

Introduction

This book tells how Rachel was born with a Language Disorder that went undiagnosed until she was 16 years old but despite struggling through mainstream education, with little or no help from professionals, she still managed to succeed against all odds.

Although initially written about events from the 1970s - 1990s, it continues to give significant insight into the difficulties encountered by children and young people with hidden language impairments. Granting that there is now more awareness of such disorders, the book is still relevant today as it becomes increasingly difficult to access professional help due to government cut backs. Rachel's type of language disorder has had many names including: Specific Language Impairment, whilst more recently being known as a Developmental Language Disorder but whatever label is used, it remains a persistent developmental condition, causing children and young people to struggle both socially and academically.

The book was initially written in the hope of inspiring parents to fight for whatever they felt their child needed. I was therefore amazed when previous editions of this book sold both nationally and internationally and proved to be essential reading on University reading lists, for people training with children and young people, especially in health care and education. It is also invaluable to those already qualified, working either professionally or voluntarily, in order to appreciate the difficulties that these children and young people face on a daily basis.

When having children, we often formulate dreams for their future around intelligence, success and material gain but I now simply wish for my children to have health, happiness and satisfaction in knowing that they have done their best for themselves and others. I am proud to be Rachel's mother and to have witnessed her triumph over all her difficulties but even more in knowing that she has helped to open the door for others.

Chapter One

We Have a Daughter

Sixteen dirty nappies a day, feeding every hour and constant screaming! And this was the baby we'd longed and planned for. Why had we bothered?

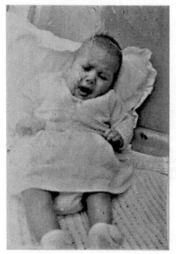 We had always dreamt of having two children; first a boy and then a little girl, so with Gary being such an easy baby it seemed only natural to have our second child when he was just 19 months old. After all, I was an experienced Registered Sick Children's Nurse who was used to coping with a ward full of other people's sick children. I therefore felt quite confident that I would be able to cope with my own offspring.

It all began at 3.15am on a fine April morning in 1972 when I woke up with what I thought was an awful stomach ache requiring nothing more than a trip to the loo! However, I soon realised how wrong I was half way down the stairs, so called for my husband Phil to help me back to bed and then sent him running off to the nearest phone box to let the hospital know that we were coming, fetch my parents from across the road to babysit for Gary and to borrow their car, as I knew I couldn't wait for the ambulance. Things were happening too fast! When he returned from his quick sprint around the block, the poor chap was sent off again to summon an ambulance urgently as it was now apparent that I was in no state to travel by car! Whilst I lay there on my own in heavy labour, intermittently biting my pillow and reassuring Gary that Mummy had only cried out because she'd had a bad dream, I reflected upon how ironic life was, as I had come across so many articles on emergency child birth during this pregnancy. Strangely enough my mind was so busy coping with the situation that I wasn't a bit worried. Instead I just kept telling myself that everything must be proceeding normally to happen so fast, because complications would only slow things down. So I just lay there, giving instructions to my little crew of amateur midwives as they arrived and trusted in God.

My father was assigned to Gary whom he soon settled and then no doubt went downstairs to make himself a cup of tea or do the traditional pacing of floors while my mother took it upon herself to reassure me that nothing would happen just yet but soon agreed with me that the head was in fact coming after a quick glance in the right direction! I was therefore more than grateful that Phil had been with me for Gary's birth and knew how to support my legs, with which my mother then assisted. It wasn't long before the baby arrived and my mother told me that we had our longed-for daughter. By now it was 3.40am; everything had happened in just 25 minutes. It all seemed too good to be true!

Personally, I still felt clinically responsible as I was aware that Rachel (the name we had chosen to use for a girl) hadn't given a full lusty cry yet, which was needed for her breathing mechanism to switch over from 'maternal' to 'independent' gear. In fact, her breathing was initially very shallow but I still didn't panic. Instead my training came to the fore as I began to stimulate her by rubbing her back and tickling the soles of her feet, after which she gave the most almighty, lusty cry and failed to stop!

There was now a dilemma about what to do about the cord that needed to be cut but I felt confident in waiting for 15 minutes. Even so, as no one had arrived from the medical world yet, I sent my team running off to boil the first drop of the traditional gallons of water often believed to be required on these occasions. I then suggested that they sterilised some clean string and a sharp pair of scissors whilst I prayed that all would go well; at the same time consoling myself that there wasn't much that could go wrong provided that I tied the cord tightly enough!

Thankfully the ambulance team chose that moment to arrive and soon summoned a Doctor and Midwife to come post-haste over their telecom system, which they did, whilst we all relaxed, leaving them to finish off the necessary details. The first thing the efficient Midwife did after cutting the cord was to point out that we had left the bedroom window open! Why had none of us noticed this? Consequently, in the days before central heating, since being thrust from a warm womb at record speed Rachel had been merely wrapped in a towel and gradually allowed to cool

13

off! I felt devastated; how could we have all have been so preoccupied that we didn't think of such a basic thing? Subsequently, to further add to my pique, she dressed Rachel, laid her in a warmed carry-cot and promptly took her downstairs to be near the open fire.

Meanwhile, after I'd been washed and settled in a freshly made bed, I was given a couple of sleeping tablets and told to sleep while everyone went downstairs with Rachel, who was still complaining at the top of her newly found voice. Before leaving, the Midwife had left instructions to feed Rachel with some sugar water at 5am if she still hadn't stopped crying, but just as they were about to prepare a bottle she suddenly stopped and went to sleep.

Now that we had our new baby daughter, I felt that our family was complete; just as we had dreamt it would be. As the day began to dawn, I decided to slip downstairs to have a peep at Rachel. After all, I hadn't even held her yet! Although I now believe that Rachel's problems were probably genetically linked, I often thought back on those events over the next few years, and wondered if her birth had caused any of her future problems. She had been thrust into the world at record speed, hadn't breathed properly for the first 1 - 2 minutes and I'd not been able to hold her for the first few hours. Later in the day I tried to breast feed Rachel but didn't expect to experience any problems. I thought she took the feed well, after which we both held her for a while before settling her in her cot. She slept for about 20 minutes but after that she just would not be pacified! In the end I tried feeding her again - after all, a lot of people believed in demand feeding in those days.

After a few days I found I was having to feed her hourly in order to prevent her from screaming but it seemed she was only quiet and happy for about 20 minutes following each feed. You could set a clock by it! We didn't know it at the time but this was to become Rachel's style of living for some time to come. Not only that, she had frequent, very loose stools. One day I counted as many as sixteen dirty nappies but the most frustrating thing was that nobody really listened or seemed to believe what I was trying to tell them or share our concerns. The Midwife simply suggested that I drank some whisky after the 6pm feed in the hope of passing it on to Rachel at the 10pm one. Now I hate spirits but I cringed

And drank it. By this stage I was prepared to try anything in order to get some sleep and have a break from that eternal crying. What was I doing wrong? I'd had plenty of experience, including having sole charge of a ward full of twenty sick babies and children, apart from coping with my own son. I'd tried every trick I knew in the book but all my Midwife and Health Visitor could suggest was to try them all again!

My energy was being sapped and I was fast running out of patience! I was also beginning to feel desperate as nothing seemed to pacify her and no one else seemed to care! When Rachel was 10 days old, we found that she had lost over 1 Kg (2lbs 4oz) in weight. By now I felt quite anxious as I could almost see her shrinking before my eyes but nobody else seemed perturbed by this. Surely this would alert the professionals to something. Instead they merely suggested that she must be allergic to my milk so told me to try bottle feeding her. I must admit that this did help things slightly as she began to gain weight and didn't need feeding quite so often but she still cried and screamed an awful lot!

I'm not sure why, but my mother seemed to think I would find it comforting to know that I had been considered a bad-tempered child until I was 2 years old, so told me so at frequent intervals but it didn't help. I only found it irritating. One day while I was in the chemist, I noticed a product called Sister Laura's something or other, which was added to feeds to thicken them and aid digestion so, as I thought anything was worth trying, I bought some. Now I don't know who Sister Laura was but I will be eternally grateful to her, because at 3 months old Rachel began to settle into 4 hourly feeds at last and even slept through the night for the first time. It was a magic formula alright.

It was also about this time that I noticed a difference in Rachel when holding her in my arms. Up until then I had felt that something was missing between us. It's hard to put into words but although I loved her, she didn't seem to respond and snuggle herself into my arms, moulding herself to me as most babies did. Instead she appeared to remain aloof; almost detached from us. Then one magical day I felt her snuggle into my arms and felt the bonding that I had been waiting for. Phil also noticed this difference but there were still other things that puzzled me about Rachel.

Now I'm afraid I need to be technical for a minute and explain that all babies are born with several reflex reactions that are all linked to survival such as sucking when something is put to their mouths. Obviously, this reflex lasts for some time but the others usually disappear after a few months as the baby starts to 'suss the world out' and decide for itself what to do. One of these reflexes is known as the Moro reflex and probably named after some clever professor who first wrote about it, even though the caveman's babies doubtless did this. It is best described as a reaction to shock as the baby throws its arms out above its head when it feels any sudden change in position or the environment (like being dropped) or as a reaction to a sudden loud noise. This reaction has usually disappeared after 3 to 6 months as the baby becomes more aware of its surroundings and begins to assess each situation separately. For some reason though Rachel continued to react like this to loud noises, especially motor bikes, until she was about 18 months old! If she was lying in her pram when a motor bike went by, not only did she throw out her arms with her head thrust back but she 'jumped' so much that she visibly left the mattress! I hated to see her so nervous whilst being totally unable to help her. I felt so inadequate, as all I could do was simply comfort her afterwards. I was also aware that Rachel would only settle for sleep if she was wrapped tightly in a shawl; like the old-fashioned swaddling clothes. I suppose this helped her to feel safe as she did in the womb.

Although I knew there was something different about Rachel, the professionals certainly weren't bothered, so I didn't want to make a fuss at this stage. Eventually we all settled into something of a routine although there were times when I felt I could cheerfully throw her out of the nearest window. (And it was usually an upstairs one that I had in mind too!) I really think I would have lost my nerve if it wasn't for Gary being such an easy child. I consoled myself that I had coped OK with him and was doing all the same things with Rachel plus drawing on all my resources gained from my training. I really didn't think I was causing her problems but nonetheless, I questioned myself frequently.

As Rachel grew, so her feeds grew bigger until she was taking a full bottle every 4 hours. At various times I tried introducing solid foods but although she took them with relish, she always ended up screaming about 20 minutes later. We were back to the old feeding problem again only in a different guise. Therefore, I'm afraid I simply postponed facing the ultimate weaning and told myself that my parent's generation had fed us on milk until we were 6 months old and we'd survived OK. It has recently been suggested that Rachel may have been lactose intolerant, but at that time I thought she just had an immature digestive system, that would right itself in time. At least she was now gaining weight but it was no good talking to anyone at the clinic as they only suggested everything that I had already tried! After all, it wasn't so long ago that I had been out this self-same advice so, whenever I told them that I had already tried that little trick, they simply told me to go away and try again! Didn't they realise that I was asking for help because I needed support. I didn't want to be placated and merely sent home again.

We carried on in this vein while Rachel was taking a full bottle every 4 hours but of course the inevitable occurred and she needed more food. I therefore started feeding her 3 hourly bottles, which she seemed to find satisfying although I knew it was wrong. By now I had tried every reliable starter baby foods and cereals but they all produced the same screaming reaction. In desperation I decided to try her on some powdered adult breakfast cereal and thank goodness we had a contented baby who waited until the next feed. Later, I offered her some breakfast biscuits mashed in milk with the same successful result. I therefore decided there and then to simply puree all our own suitable foods for her, rather than use commercial products, which worked extremely well until she was able to eat the usual toddler diet and ultimately normal food.

Another problem with Rachel was that she seemed to need an awful lot of entertaining, stimulating and reassurance, to get through the day. Unless I could keep her occupied, she cried. Phil therefore built her a mobile to stand over her carry cot, from which he suspended lots of strings so that I could tie on, and keep changing, a selection of different objects to keep her amused. I used everything I could think of from toys to milk bottle tops and colourful kitchen utensils like a tea strainer. As she grew older it seemed that she had to be able to see me or she'd cry. It got to the stage when, after waking up in the morning to feed, wash and dress her, I would simply shut her in her room until I had completed all the essential morning tasks, including preparing the dinner so that I'd only got to switch on the gas at the required time. I got this down to about half an hour while Gary amused himself happily with his toys and I charged around the house like grease lightning. Of course, I felt guilty hearing her wailing away upstairs but it was the only way I could cope with her and the housework. After I'd finished, we all went out for a walk to the shops to help us calm down. Fortunately, Gary appeared to be oblivious to all this and seemed to accept that babies just cried a lot anyway. For the rest of the day I would carry her about or keep her with me until Phil came home. Meanwhile, my mother continued to reassure me that I had been a bad-tempered baby until I was 2 years old but I still didn't find this very helpful, although I did pray that Rachel would reach that magical age soon!

When she could sit up, I tried sitting her in her play pen surrounded by toys whilst doing some chores but she started crying every time I passed by if I didn't stop and stay with her. Subsequently, I worked out a strategy whereby, if she was happily amusing herself for 5 minutes I would sneak out of the back door and in through the front door rather than risk going through the lounge and creating another bawling match. I really couldn't believe that I had sunk to such depths of inadequacy. Why couldn't I cope with this particular child of mine?

When Rachel was 6 months old, I was surprisingly offered an appointment with a Paediatrician and decided to use this to discuss our concerns but was duly informed by this eminent, professional consultant that I had a bad-tempered baby whom I had to learn to control, before she learnt to control me. Needless to say, I found this piece of advice just about as useful as my mother's well-worn adage!

Chapter Two

The Early Years

Both children appeared to develop normally and reach their necessary milestones at the right times. Although Gary suffered from continual ear  infections and several other health problems, he always remained a very placid and amiable child. He needed to be with his sister as she was! He also loved language and was extremely articulate and chatty. As Gary obviously enjoyed playing with multi-syllable words, I made a point of consciously trying to introduce new ones into our conversations each week. Consequently, by the time he began attending playschool he was happily discussing things like condensation and evaporation, simply because he found them interesting subjects. Gary was also a natural pacifist so, although he did nothing to protect himself or his own rights, he was a fierce defender of his little sister if anyone tried to hurt her.

Rachel however was extremely healthy but continued to be bad tempered; screaming and throwing frequent tantrums for no apparent reason! By now, I was beginning to console myself with my mother's oft repeated phrase, *"Well you were bad-tempered until you were 2 years old"* but I stopped going to the clinic as I only felt frustrated when they were unable to help me.

By the time Rachel reached that long-awaited age of 2 years old she began to take an interest in picture books but for some reason she always held the book upside down! Even when we corrected her, she would reverse it again as if to say 'this is the way I see it best thank you!' Although her language seemed to develop at a reasonable rate, I noticed that despite having a good vocabulary she didn't always use the words in the right places. But I thought this was just immature speech that would eventually correct itself. After all Gary had been advanced in speech but slow to

Walk whereas Rachel had launched herself at 10 months old but been slower to talk.

When Gary entered school aged 5 years he was already beginning to read and write and took to school like a duck to water. I therefore had more time to observe Rachel but the more I noticed the more puzzled I became. By that time, I was an assistant at her playschool and noticed that when personally guided by an adult Rachel loved to do jigsaws puzzles or sticking. However, when left to her own devices, she generally preferred to just run repeatedly around the large pieces of apparatus, occasionally going on the slide but then proceeding to frantically charge around in circles again. I was also intrigued by Rachel's choice of friends as she seemed to gravitate towards children that were either younger than her, generally described as being 'odd' or would probably need special education. However, I did nothing to stop this as I felt it was important for her to develop some friendships of her own. Even at home she still didn't appear to want to play with toys and lacked any imaginative play, so it was still difficult to keep her amused.

When Rachel was 4 years old, I thought it was time that she knew her colours but despite all our efforts she still continued to use random colour names when she thought a label was required. So, one day when we were alone, I decided to sit down with her to see whether or not she was colour blind. I collected together lots of bricks and various other red, green, yellow and blue objects in a range of subtle shades to see if she could group them. I reckon she could have done it standing on her head! She had no problem at all. It was obviously the labelling process that was causing her difficulties.

After that I became aware of all the other oddities in her language. Unlike Gary's love of new words being introduced into his vocabulary, Rachel flatly refused to try repeating a new word. Furthermore, if we tried to show and explain something to her, thinking she would find it interesting, she always closed her eyes, and said, "*I can't see it!*" Another little trick she developed was to avoid describing things by always showing us or demonstrating, tending to point and say "*that,*" "*there,*" "*this one*" or "*those,*" rather than use a noun (naming word) or preposition (position word). Rachel also confused words like 'eat' and 'drink.' or 'hot' and 'cold.' One day when visiting a travelling fairground for a family outing, she indicated that she wanted a toffee apple but being independent she typically insisted on purchasing this for herself. Regrettably though, this only resulted in bitter tears when Rachel unwittingly asked the stall holder for a "candy floss," which of course he gave her. As any attempts to correct Rachel's errors resulted in terrible tantrums, we tended to just repeat correctly what we thought she meant. Sometimes this still caused a scene if she insisted on using her word: but we got by. As long as we did the right thing and not necessarily what she said. Although this could become quite confusing at times as can be imagined. In fact, it was all a matter of compromise in an attempt to avoid any unnecessary frustration tantrums.

It was about this time that my mother began to acknowledge that Rachel might be a bit more difficult than I had been. By now, my nerves and stamina were stretched to their limits and it took all my strength to stay in control of the situation. In truth, I was secretly beginning to wonder how long I'd be able to control her. Even if I succeeded now while she was 4 years old, I dreaded to think what she would be like as a teenager!

One of her least endearing habits was the way she found a hundred and one ways of saying the same thing over and over again. This was particularly difficult to cope with at 5am in the morning, when we were hoping for a lie in! She would start off by calling out all our names and telling us individually that she was awake. As if we hadn't noticed! She would then go on to say, *"I'm not asleep. Are you asleep Gary?"* Following this she would then proceed to work her way through us all again by asking us all the same question individually. And so she would continue until either Phil or I told her, in no uncertain terms, to be quiet! Regrettably, this didn't last for very long as she couldn't amuse herself and craved companionship or entertainment. She still needed our constant company when awake and unfortunately for us, she needed very little sleep.

One of the most difficult things to cope with for both Rachel and us was her tremendous fear of anything that she didn't understand or thought was beyond her control. The world must have been very frightening for her as she needed to trust both the people close to her and the actual objects around her in order to feel safe. For example, Rachel loved her inflatable Mickey Mouse toy that had always been fully inflated and ready for play since her first birthday, until one day it developed a puncture. When she realised that it had changed its size and shape, she wouldn't go near it, not even after Phil had repaired the puncture and blown it up again. As she didn't understand what had happened she didn't trust it any more. Any attempts to bring it near her resulted in real terror so we had to give it away. After that all inflatable objects were treated with the same distrust.

Another real fear for her was sand, which was a shame as we lived near the beach. I can only assume that she also felt insecure on this as it didn't feel as solid as the land she was used to standing on in the garden or on the pavements. Therefore, as a baby we coped by simply leaving her to play in her pushchair, gradually progressing to sitting her on our laps and in due course, a blanket. Eventually she ventured onto the sand herself wearing shoes and by the time she was 5 years old she was able to play on the firm wet sand in bare feet; slowly moving on to the drier stuff as her confidence grew. However, this was relatively easy to cope with compared to moving water such as the sea or rivers. That took the patience of a saint; and one with ear muffs too due to all the screaming!

Sudden load noises still remained a problem for her as well. Whenever an aeroplane flew overhead, no matter how high in the sky, Rachel would run indoors and motorbikes proved to be a constant problem as they were always there on the road when we walked along the pavement. If Rachel came remotely near a motorbike, either on the road or even in the display window of a garage or shop she would 'freeze' and go ram rod stiff. On these occasions the only way we could pass by was to carry her, which was not easy when she was so stiff that she couldn't bend. The motorbike problem was also compounded by the fact that a crash helmet represented a motorbike to her. After all, she didn't know which bit might make that awful noise! Consequently, as her own grandfather rode a motorbike, Rachel would refuse to enter their lounge if his crash helmet was on the table. Furthermore, if he ever walked into the room wearing it, she immediately hid behind a chair. She was absolutely petrified.

Even Father Christmas became such a phobia that he had to be sent a note one year asking him to leave any toys or presents for our house in the garden shed before she would relax and go to sleep. She wasn't letting any strange man come down her chimney in the middle of the night! We did try to warn her playgroup leader prior to their Christmas party but she told us not to worry as she would cope. After all, many children were either

Nonetheless, I don't think she was quite prepared for the amount of panic that Rachel displayed when Santa arrived. She often spoke of this for many years, describing how Rachel had literally leapt onto her lap and sat there quivering like a leaf. It took years of effort and patience to gradually desensitise Rachel from each fear individually but I'm afraid a lot had to wait until she was about 8 years old when her language and reasoning ability had improved enough for her to understand more of the world in general.

Unfortunately, it was about this time that her eating habits became a major issue yet again. Following the age-old advice, I started off by ignoring it but it quickly became apparent that if Rachel had her way, she would only eat her pudding but no dinner and only cake for tea, having ignored the first course. Breakfast was the only meal that she would eat normally. I therefore decided to start saying, *"Well, if you can't eat your dinner you can't be very hungry so there's no pudding."* We also used the same policy at tea time but I soon realised that as she was as strong as us, she simply ended up going without the meal. As we thought that hunger would be bound to win over in the end, we even stopped her milk and biscuits in between meals so she just drank water. We didn't make an issue of it or even try to discuss it with her; we just quietly removed her plate and waited for the next meal. This continued for a fortnight, after which I began to worry as I was afraid her health would begin to suffer if I let her carry on like that. We therefore tried giving her the most miniscule meal of a teaspoonful of mince, a teaspoonful of mashed potato and literally one pea and one piece of diced carrot or equivalent. I then insisted that she ate it all - even though this could take up to 2 hours!

I must admit that I did at times resort to force feeding her but she just ran up to the front door or into the toilet to make herself sick. Now this did upset Gary. He'd coped admirably with all her fears, frustration and temper tantrums. He didn't resent the extra attention she seemed to get at these times, as I always made a point of talking it through with him afterwards and giving him some extra time as well, but he hated seeing me being forceful with her. I hated it too but I was worried that her stomach was beginning to adjust to just one meal a day. This pattern did eventually break but only after many battles and lots of heartbreak and tears from both of us. She was so strong willed but we believed it would be detrimental to

23

her both physically and mentally to let her win this particular battle. Rachel remained a difficult eater until she was about 8 years old but many years later, I learnt that not only did she have an orthodontic problem but that children with her language disorder often had eating difficulties as well. However, all I knew at that time was that I had a difficult child and according to the Paediatrician, I was supposed to win.

One day when Rachel was about 4 years old, I decided to write a synopsis of her life to date in an old note book and then, in desperation to try and work out what I was dealing with, I used my nursing analytical skills to list all the identified problems individually. I then decided to prioritise them in order of what we needed to deal with first and began to develop a plan of action, to try and help her overcome them. In this way I began a systematic method of monthly reviews on her development and problems, while also reviewing and updating the plan. I also entered any other unusual events in the diary whether they were good or bad. At that time I found these diaries a good cathartic exercise for myself as well as being helpful in trying to analyse and understand Rachel's problems but subsequently, they also assisted me when I wrote my first book on Rachel.

Chapter Three

School Begins

When Rachel began full time school, at 5 years of age, I was concerned that she wasn't really ready to start formal education but as I knew all the  children would be at different stages of readiness, I hoped she would be able to fit in somewhere. After all, she was keen to start and that was the main thing, as she thought she would then be clever like Gary and learn to read and write. In order to prepare her for this we had taken her along to all the big school functions like concerts, fetes and sports days to familiarise her with the place. We had even watched the children running around at play-time so at least there would be no fear of the unexpected in that area. It was also a small school consisting of just three classrooms, with only thirteen pupils in her reception class, so I simply braced myself and hoped that she would soon settle in and cope with whatever was expected of her.

The first day seemed to go reasonably well although the teacher did tell me that Rachel had refused to draw a picture when asked. Oh dear, I knew that she was strong minded but hadn't imagined she'd be that strong willed in such a setting! On reflection I could see that Rachel had purely been trying to protect herself from humiliation but unfortunately her teacher hadn't realised this; kind though this lady was. Have you ever tried explaining such a thing to your child's teacher? How often are we the parents, who after all are supposed to know our children best, merely labelled as being over-protective, over-aspiring or even fussy parents if we dare to explain our child's point of view? Well I didn't want that to happen on her first day so I respectfully reiterated the expected phrase to the teacher and told Rachel that she really should try to do as asked.

Seemingly all the children were asked to draw a picture of themselves but Rachel decided to play safe by drawing a picture of her house instead, but of course this again was a typically primitive child style house, so her teacher was not too pleased! Furthermore, when reminded of what she was supposed to have drawn and sent back to do just that, Rachel had known it was beyond her ability - so refused. Not the best start!

As time went on, we couldn't see any real change in her from playschool. She continued to draw all her pictures on the back of cards and folders and still wrote her name back to front in reverse mirror image, starting with the l, with all the letters correctly formed but facing the wrong way. She was also slow to learn to read. We therefore went along to Rachel's first parents' evening hoping to discuss our concerns regarding these intriguing little enigmas. I was sure that something wasn't quite right as she seemed so bright in so many ways and was even more alert than Gary at times. We looked at all the children's paintings displayed on the wall, each one accompanied by their writing, but Rachel's simply consisted of a painted blue blob on a large piece of paper with what appeared to be an 'a,' 'c' and 't' arranged haphazardly around the blob. It seemed that this was the sum total of her writing skills developed after one term at school. Under the painting her teacher had written 'This is Rachel's Daddy's car.' She was the only child who hadn't done her own writing and we hadn't even been able to recognise her attempt of our car, even though we knew it was blue. When we asked the teacher what she thought was causing Rachel's problems she dismissed our concerns by describing Rachel as 'a highly-strung child who was taking longer than usual to settle in.' We also learnt that she was constantly running into her brother's adjoining class-room throughout the day to see him, so assumed that she needed to do this for reassurance and security in much the same way that she had craved my presence as a baby.

However, when it came to the Christmas concert Rachel was in her element and excelled herself by taking the part of Little Miss Muffet and singing a solo verse whilst alone on stage. She knew the nursery rhyme well and was full of confidence in situations like this. What a complex creature she was!

Rachel's fears and frustrations continued to cause us problems and if anything, the temper tantrums were getting stronger and longer. Very often she would try to tell us something but we'd misunderstand. Such situations would immediately be followed by, *"You don't know what I mean,"* after which she would burst into tears and sob, sometimes for as long as 20 -30 minutes. I found it best at these times to just sit on the floor with her on my lap, hold her tight and rock back and forth until the storm abated. We would then try again to gently work out what she was trying to say. Sometimes though, there was no containing her and she would simply lie on the floor thrashing her arms and legs about until she exhausted herself. Interestingly Rachel kept these exhibitions of frustration private within the family home so my mother and others found it hard to believe that she behaved in this way, until they actually witnessed it for themselves.

One day my mother was trying to explain how to play a simple card game to Rachel but when she found this too hard to understand, Rachel simply threw the whole pack of cards at her grandmother, who subsequently discovered how strong Rachel could be when trying to make her pick them up again. Another time Rachel threw all the cushions from the three-piece suite onto the floor and refused to pick them up. On another occasion, she became so frustrated because she couldn't understand something, that she angrily pushed her doll's pram so forcefully, that it flew from one end of the hall, over the polished floor and straight through the fully glazed front door at the other end, causing glass to shatter everywhere! By now, my mother was beginning to believe me about Rachel being difficult but to most people she just portrayed herself as a shy, quiet, little 'wallflower' who, if asked a question, generally replied with, *"Yes," "No"* or *"I don't know,"* if out of her depth in a conversation, thus giving the appearance of not being very bright. I knew that I was dealing with something beyond my own capabilities but felt frustrated because, although we were barely coping, no one else seemed to either listen or believe us. To say that Rachel was an unreasonable child is rather harsh but the fact remained that she could not be reasoned with. Although she always appeared to listen to an explanation as to why she couldn't do something, she always replied with the same answer, *"I know but I want to!"*

One of the few things that Rachel found enjoyable was dancing and had always instinctively moved to music from an early age. We initially took her along to an unambitious group that simply danced for pleasure and produced the occasional show but, in spite of her difficulties, Rachel set herself high targets and quickly wanted to change to a dancing school that used barres and *"spoke French."* Goodness knows why when she found

English so hard but I think she had been inspired by a romantic children's series on TV about a girl at ballet school. I found it very difficult to find a sympathetic teacher in the district who had high standards but didn't push students through examinations but eventually found one in the next town. Luckily, Rachel's best friend Heather, who as usual was one year younger, began at the same time which gave Rachel some support for her first visits.

By the time Rachel was 6 ½ years old I was all but dragging her to school sobbing every day. Sometimes she even went so far as to complain of a sore throat but on taking her to the Doctor, I was told that she was perfectly alright; she was just skiving from school. By now Rachel was in the top infant class and being prepared for Junior School but she was by no means ready for this. However, every time I tried to speak to anyone about the problems that I thought she had, I was simply told that she was alright and that there were plenty of other children like Rachel in the school, which only made me feel patronised - and it certainly didn't help! Maybe there were plenty of other children with her lack of ability but were they all as upset by their lack of achievement? How many others were being dragged to school sobbing each day and displaying such frustration tantrums? Anyway, they were *their* parent's problems and Rachel was ours; to cope with alone it seemed from the amount of support we'd received from either the health or educational professionals!

Even Rachel's play appeared to be different from that of other children. She was fixated on playing 'Mummies and Babies,' which simply meant enacting out everyday circumstances as she still had little imaginative play. Even though she was good at doing jigsaws, she was reluctant to play with any other toys. It seemed as though she didn't know how to play properly. I later learnt that a child needs to have a good knowledge of language before being able to play, especially imaginatively. I'm afraid meal times were still an ongoing problem as she didn't appear to enjoy eating. By now it seemed to have become a matter of principle that, rightly or wrongly, had developed, into a battle of wills. I often felt guilty - but with no professional advice we merely continued to do what we thought best, which was for Rachel to eat the miniscule meal provided, however long it took.

Although they were diminishing as her understanding grew, Rachel's fears and phobias were still present, including her extraordinary degree of fear in any new situation. Sometimes she even lacked confidence in people that we thought she trusted, like the family of her other close friend Linda who lived a few doors away. Now Linda and Rachel almost lived together, eating and playing in each other's houses but although Linda often slept over with us, Rachel could not bring herself to sleep in Linda's house. One night when this was tried Rachel went to bed in Linda's house but left and came home to sleep at about 8.30pm, going back for breakfast as soon as she was awake! If this very kind family invited Rachel to go with them on an outing, Rachel would only go if they took Gary as well or I went along instead. She couldn't even walk the few doors up the road to Linda's house alone when she wanted to go there to play.

By now, Rachel had somehow managed to achieve a reasonable reading age at school but she still read some words backwards like "let" for 'tell' or "saw" for 'was' but nothing distressed her more than having to write a story. Rachel lived in dread of story writing each school day as she usually only managed to write about three lines, after which she always printed THE END in large block capitals as if to say 'that's all I'm doing!' In actual fact, none of her class work was ever finished.

On looking in her school books I could see that about half her writing was still mirrored and this extended into number work as well, writing 12 as 21 along with reversing her number shapes. Consequently, a lot of her work was marked wrong when in fact her mental calculations were actually correct, which obviously caused her great distress. Rachel knew that she had to work hard to improve her "*untidy handwriting*" as she called it but to mark her sums wrong when she knew they were right seemed like a gross injustice to her.

I'm afraid her art work was still very immature with her drawings consisting of either a primitively drawn house or girl, while all cards and folders continued to be illustrated on the back but sadly, Rachel was now becoming self-conscious of her creative work. I remember one day she came home very distressed because she was the only child in the class not to have a project folder. Apparently, the whole class had been growing cress in an egg shell, which Rachel had really enjoyed, coming home and telling us little bits about it. When it was time to do the written work, the teacher gave them all a folder in which to keep their work and asked them to illustrate the front cover; so of course, Rachel drew her picture on the back. The teacher took the folder away and placed another in front of Rachel the correct way around but she promptly turned it over and drew on the back again. The teacher told me that she did this three times, after which she thought Rachel was being obstinate so refused to give her a fourth folder.

I think the more that was asked of Rachel in school the more she failed, so just like the first day at school, she tried to avoid the humiliation of failure. If she'd had the courage, I think she might have opted out of school but thankfully she was blessed with great determination instead and a strong will to succeed. I also noticed that Rachel was a rather clumsy child at home, often spilling the milk when pouring it over her cereal in the morning unless I put it in a small cream jug to save her starting the day with yet another failure. She was useless at ball games; preferring to duck rather than try to catch the ball, no matter how large or small or how near or gently thrown to her. She couldn't skip with a skipping rope and although she loved dancing, she had great difficulty in remembering a simple sequence of steps. Indeed, I really don't know how she coped with dancing as she couldn't repeat a simple rhythm when clapped and I was convinced by her singing at this stage that she was probably tone deaf!

Her language was still not developing as we'd hoped either. Most people thought she was just shy because of the way she avoided entering into conversations with others or just gave very brief or simple answers. She had however, grown into quite a pretty girl and discovered that she could often get by quite easily by being coy with men. Those eyes could be quite amazing at times! At home she spoke quite freely with us but her words were often muddled or swapped around. She would even use word substitutes like calling Girl Guides, "*blue brownies*" and hearing aids, "*deaf boxes.*" One day she said, "*I've swutched the rectangle on*" by which she meant 'I've switched the radio off!' If we ever tried to talk or explain something to her, she would either simply walk off while we were in mid-sentence or act like a stupid little idiot, going all giggly and behaving in such a ridiculous fashion so that the conversation became impossible.

Retrospectively, it seems amazing to look back on all this and realise that we had just let things ride along at their own pace for so long but I had been told so many times by GPs, Paediatricians, Health Visitors, teachers and even friends and family that they all felt there was nothing wrong with Rachel, she was no different from many other children, she was just bad-tempered or strong willed and I was constantly reminded that we all muddle our words at times. Simultaneously we were also coping with Gary's health problems, including fortnightly ear infections with nine perforated ear drums, being investigated for TB and even cancer along with his excessive bruising for minor injuries. Furthermore, his teachers and his Cub Leaders were all asking the same questions about Gary's bruising that we had already asked a the Doctors but our GP simply dismissed it as being 'boyish war wounds,' while casualty questioned us for physical child abuse! However, if I ever asked for a blood test, I was made to feel that I was being neurotic, so I began to believe this too. Several years later when Gary was 12 years old, we discovered that he had been born with Haemophilia but only after he'd bled excessively at home and taken about a month to heal following some minor dental extractions to help straighten his teeth.

Perhaps you can now imagine how I was feeling. I was constantly questioning my own gut feelings and began thinking that I was the one with the problem, not my children. Social services questioned us about Gary's bruising, the health professionals thought I was a fussy mother and the school said we were pushy parents expecting too much from our daughter. I therefore tried to believe in all these professional people and to accept Gary and Rachel as they were. Nonetheless, deep down I knew that this was not true. I knew in my heart that Rachel had a problem but no one else seemed to believe me. At times I tried to explain things to my sister who always listened but was at a loss when it came to helping me, apart from allowing me to cry out my frustrations on her shoulder, which may have helped me but didn't change a thing for Rachel.

Ironically, my sister had always looked upon me as the expert in the family when it came to child care, yet here I was, blatantly not coping with my own! One thing she had noticed though was how I seemed to treat my children differently if disciplining them. Not that Gary needed much correction as he always responded well to a reasonable explanation but I was very aware that whenever Rachel threw one of her tantrums or began sobbing, I literally felt myself switch into what I can only describe as clinical mode. I remember thinking 'Here we go again,' and physically feel a change in my attitude because, if I'd stayed in my natural emotional manner, I think I would have simply joined in rather than cope with her problems. I always felt that no one could really have as many individual problems in life as Rachel seemed to have; surely they all stemmed from one cause? If only we could make sense of it all and discover what that was.

Meanwhile, I tried working out a programme of activities that might help her, beginning with her hand-eye coordination along with her general physical skills that I knew were poor. We worked hard at skipping and hopping which she enjoyed as she was keen to be able to skip like her peers and she loved playing hopscotch, but at that stage she still couldn't catch a ball when it was all but placed in her hands. At the slightest hint of a throw from anything more than 6 inches (15cm) away she would duck and shield her face. Gradually, in gentle stages, we progressed to using smaller balls, being thrown over a larger distance and eventually moved on to bat and ball games. Although her ability to catch a ball made relatively slow progress, I was amazed at how well Rachel responded and how quickly she learnt when we started with the basics and broke everything down into easy stages for her.

I also read as many books on learning difficulties that I could find and understand. By doing this I came across a few recommended activity books, some of which involved drawing a lot of lines from left to right and tracing. Surprisingly, Rachel did not find these too boring. Instead she actually seemed to enjoy the challenge and was openly grateful and relieved to know that at least we acknowledged that she had a problem and wanted to help her.

By helping out at a local school and reading lots of library books I had learnt about the importance of body control in large and fine motor (physical) activities but first the child had to really understand its own body and how it related to its surroundings. For example, the child has to know that its head and body are joined by its neck. The understanding of left and right is also important. Even if the child doesn't know the different names it needs to decide on a dominant hand and to be able to distinguish between what is on this side of the room and what is on that side. Otherwise, how can a child be expected to learn that 'c' is followed by 'a' which is followed by 't' to spell 'cat' in the left to right pattern, if it doesn't

Understand left from right? Likewise, how can a child learn about positioning short and tall letters on or under the line without fully understanding the meaning of under and over? I therefore began to realise that in order to learn to read and write, children not only had to recognise shapes but also understand how everyday objects related to each other.

To teach her this we encouraged her to play with lots of big cardboard boxes in the garden and to climb over all sorts of playground apparatus whilst constantly talking to her about on, under, over and through, etc. Furthermore, Rachel had no understanding of left or right whatsoever and used either hand to point, eat or pick things up. She also had no understanding of how the objects around her related to each other, so couldn't say 'The cup on the table' or 'Under the chair.'

Nevertheless, she was determined herself to overcome all her difficulties as she hated being called 'stupid' by other children and thankfully responded well to our structured style of teaching through play. Dancing was another fun way to not only reinforce left and right but also good practice for learning sequences and helping to remember what came next; even if this did entail me going along to the lesson every so often to learn the new dance as well, so that I could help her practice at home. Rachel was so keen that she insisted on practicing at home morning, afternoon and evening until she could do it without me prompting her.

It was this degree of determination to succeed that gave us the strength and motivation to help her although it was very demanding along with all the other chores and commitments involved in family life.

Chapter Four

Time for Strategies

After Rachel had settled into main stream school, I was lucky enough to secure a job as a teaching assistant in a Unit for Children with Impaired Hearing. The work mainly involved helping the deaf children to integrate with their hearing peers in the classroom and my experience there was to prove invaluable in helping Rachel. It was while working there that I met Julie, a trained Speech and Language Therapist and Teacher of the Deaf, who became a very good friend as we discovered that we had the same sense of humour, held similar views on many different subjects and enjoyed the same hobbies. Before being employed at the Unit Julie had worked at a School for Children with Language Disorders. I found her an interesting person and we spent many lunch hours just chatting and generally putting the world to rights.

One day while talking to Julie, I poured out my feelings of frustrations and confusion over Rachel and was surprised to find that she was the first person to really understand and believe me; not only that, she had met Rachel so knew her to be a bright little thing and didn't try to patronise me. In fact, Julie offered to assess Rachel for me! Now I hadn't been expecting that so felt both embarrassed and confused but she explained that part of her training had involved learning how to assess a child's language and some other areas of development. I didn't know what to say. As much as I wanted to have an assessment done, I didn't want to give Julie the embarrassment of telling a friend that she was neurotic and that her daughter was fine, just as everyone else seemed to believe. Julie went on to explain that if we didn't want to accept her offer, we had the right as parents, to ask our local Educational Psychologist, Kevin Brown to examine Rachel and that the school couldn't stop us. I felt extremely grateful to Julie for her offer of help but asked if I could wait and discuss it over with Phil before giving her our answer.

That evening Phil and I discussed all this at some length as it was not an easy decision to make. Although we were sorely tempted to accept Julie's offer of help, as we knew and trusted her implicitly, we didn't want to put her in a difficult situation. At the same time, I knew that Kevin Brown was a well-liked and respected man who worked with the children with hearing impairment and often came into the Unit. In the end we decided to ask Kevin to do the assessment and wrote a polite letter to Rachel's school informing them of our decision.

That was in March, but as I knew there was a long waiting list to see Kevin we decided to continue with our own programme of activities in the meantime. Rachel had now finished the first set of books in which she'd practiced tracing from left to right and had moved on to some other remedial books that she seemed to enjoy just as much. Another thing we'd been recommended to try was the new video game, fast becoming a craze, involving a game of tennis on TV. By sitting on the left of the screen and controlling the player on the left-hand side, Rachel had to watch the ball going from left to right, which was meant to reinforce the eye movements needed for reading and writing in a fun way. At first, she was absolutely hopeless at this and had no idea of how to handle the control but as usual, when taught in small, structured steps, she quickly became quite proficient.

We also joined the local toy library that enabled both Gary and Rachel to play with all the educational toys available in the cheapest possible way. One of the first things we borrowed was a big wooden posting box that used very specific shapes such as a cross with two fat and two thin arms that could only be posted in one way. I thought this was ideal to help Rachel learn to recognise the specific direction of shape that she'd need with letters. Although she found this quite difficult, she liked playing with it as she enjoyed a challenge. One day when we had all the pieces spread out over the lounge carpet, feeling and talking about the different shapes, my Mother arrived and walked into the room but immediately started crying to see her 7 year old grand-daughter playing with a baby's toy. I remember telling her to get out if she couldn't cope and not bothering to come back until she'd sorted herself out! I explained that if she preferred seeing Rachel as she was and watching her suffer, she could leave, as I was prepared to do everything necessary to help her.

Needless to say, it hurt me too, that my daughter still couldn't play with such basic toys competently but I was glad to find anything suitable that could help her and be used as part of her training. I was always inspired by Rachel's own motivation and the way she learnt so quickly when we used a step by step, touch and feel approach. However, as we thought it best to leave her to cope with schoolwork during the term, we left our programme of remedial books and games for the holidays, in the hope of easing Rachel's problems and frustrations until the Educational Psychologist could see her. We knew that he was very busy and that it would be a long time before her appointment but we were sure it would be worth it in the end. At least we would then have an honest and unbiased opinion at last.

Sadly, we felt unable to help Rachel with many of her other problems like refusing to join in educational type conversations, the way she muddled her words, not being able to explain things or her unaccountable, amazing fear of unknown situations. I well remember one trip to a popular picnic area, known locally as the gibbet due to its past history, where there were some chalk cliffs, down which most children loved to slide, climb back up and slide down again. Some even brought metal trays with them specifically for this purpose while others simply wore holes in their trousers! We had dressed our children in hardy old play clothes, as had my sister who was coming with us along with her 3 year old son Brett. Now I'm afraid Rachel saw danger in nearly everything Brett did and was so over-protective of him that I'm surprised the poor little chap didn't lash out at her in frustration. We later decided to do the cliff path walk around the perimeter of the area, which really alarmed Rachel. Even my sister was amazed at the degree of Rachel's fear as she hadn't witnessed her in such a state before. Not only did she scream and sob most of the way round, she 'froze' to the spot refusing to walk and held herself so ram rod stiff that she couldn't bend, making it very difficult for Phil to carry her.

Eventually, after about 6 weeks of the aforementioned holiday activities, we began to see an improvement in Rachel. At first, we noticed that although her pictures still displayed a basic house and primitive people, she was beginning to add trees and flowers. She still had difficulty in copying some shapes but was beginning to try drawing animals and made a very good attempt of drawing a cat sitting down. She still didn't finish a picture when colouring in but her handwriting was certainly improving, in spite of her lack of finger spaces or word grouping. She was definitely trying to help herself. By now Rachel had become quite accomplished at the video game and was well aware of her right hand, which she tried hard to use consistently. I even noticed her correcting herself if she used her left hand by mistake. All of which reinforced our belief in that we were right to help Rachel and encouraged us to continue with our planned programme in spite of what others thought of us.

It was in late April when we really noticed a big change in Rachel though. One day we were sitting at a table looking at a book together, when we came across a picture of some native American Indians complete with feathered head-dresses. It was a week before my birthday and she couldn't have given me a better present if she'd spent a million pounds. Rachel actually asked me a question about the Indians! She didn't manage to phrase the question properly but by pointing and the intonation of her voice I could tell that she wanted to know something about them wearing feathers in their hair. I answered as simply as I could, as if answering a 2 year old. She listened and accepted the reply but ended the conversation there. I cannot explain how I felt; I wanted to shout for joy, say a prayer of thanks, go out in the street to dance and hug the first person who came along. All at once, if that was possible! Rachel had asked her first question and I was both relieved and delighted even though she was 7 years old!

After that she began to query lots of different words that she heard us use in general conversation like 'logical 'or 'pollution.' I don't think she always understood our answers, even when given the simplest of explanations but she wasn't put off and continued to ask more questions; even if they confused me at times. I remember one day she asked "*Is Australia in England Mummy?*" I was ecstatic at the daily changes and improvements that we saw in her. It was as though she was really starting to open the door to understanding and learning. Only a few weeks before I had been in despair of her totally closed mind but now it was slowly opening and was fantastic to see.

During the Easter holidays Rachel showed real enthusiasm in helping Phil and Gary plant seeds in our back garden. Gary had always taken great delight in having his own little plot of land since he was a toddler and had now progressed to helping with the main vegetable crop for the family. Rachel had always been offered the same experience but refused to join in until now. Still, it seemed this year was different. Phil was just as amazed and excited as I was at the way she reacted when shown the seeds.

In fact, he said she even looked around to find more and maintained an interest when asked, 'How many?' Responding by counting the seeds in her hand. Moreover, she continued watching the seeds' development over the following weeks, which was real progress for us.

Rachel continued to ask several questions each day, appearing to be ready to learn at last, but as the school holiday grew to a close her words became more muddled again, climaxing in terrible moods, tantrums and regressing into her own peculiar, type of stupid behaviour for the last couple of days. I could only assume that this was due to her anxiety about going back to school. Over the first few days of the new term Rachel seemed to be tense and irritable but was pleased to tell us that she had achieved a much better standard of work. She said that she'd managed to finish three pieces of work rather than her usual one and completed seven lines of writing instead of her usual three. I couldn't wait to see her teacher to see if this was true. As she was now back at school, we stopped our activity programme as we didn't want to overtire her or clash with her schoolwork although we did encourage any play that reinforced our holiday projects.

The next major problem for Rachel was Brownies. Now this wasn't our idea as we had enough challenges in our day to day life but Rachel had always wanted to join and often spoke of Brownies and 'Blue Brownies' as she called the Guides. Her brother was already a keen Cub collecting lots of badges down his arm and she couldn't wait to emulate him. We guessed that this would be difficult for her but as she was so keen, we decided to give it a try. After all she had lots of surplus energy to burn, was a determined little madam and we had found a way of coping with dancing. We therefore put her name down on the waiting list for a pack whose Brown Owl was a personal friend of the family and had known Rachel since she was a baby. We thought it best not to anticipate the event too early, knowing the state she could get herself into but she remembered it herself the night before and therefore became upset. Even though this was her idea, she spent all night dreaming, crying and worrying about the unknown. I think she was aware of her own limitations and was afraid she wouldn't be able to do something when asked but in spite of everything, she still wanted to go! Perverse creature that she was, it seemed she was determined to be a Brownie even though she was scared of yet another unknown situation.

At the eleventh hour she began saying that she didn't want to go to Brownies that night but would start next week instead. No way did I think the family could cope with that performance again so I'm afraid it was a case of now or never! I therefore decided that it was in all our best interests to force her. I felt torn inside between doing something that deep down I knew was probably best for her but also cruel as she cried and clung to me all the way there. I pushed her there on my bicycle as she was unable to walk and prayed that Viv, our friend the Brown Owl, would understand my philosophy. However, I felt as though the Gods were working against me though that night as Viv was late and her assistant, who was a stranger to us, was starting the meeting. Still, I thought it best to see this thing through having come so far already, so made a snap decision to sit down to watch and wait until Viv arrived. When she finally came, I gave Viv a run down on the situation, promised to go straight home and sit by the 'phone in case she needed me, told Rachel that she must try it this week but need never go back again if she didn't like it and proceeded to peel Rachel off me to make a quick getaway. On arriving home, I felt both sick and exhausted. The scene had been more like a reluctant child being dragged into the classroom

on her first day at school, rather than a child starting what was meant to be a voluntary club designed for youngsters to enjoy.

A quarter of an hour before Brownies ended, I was back there ready to meet her expecting a limp, exhausted child to emerge with a tear stained face. Instead Rachel strolled out beaming from ear to ear saying, *"I want to go again Mummy."* With the security and support from our friend Viv, Rachel did enjoy Brownies although there were a few hiccups later when Viv resigned from being Brown Owl and Rachel had to adjust to a new leader.

Badges were another a problem as once again, she set herself high targets. Rachel was not content to simply attend and enjoy the weekly meetings.

Oh no! She had to have as many badges as, if not more than, the best of them. This clearly made it difficult for us, as we obviously didn't want to quench her enthusiasm, but it did mean we had to choose all her badges carefully, so that she could present most of her work as being completed on the day of the test. We also tried to ensure that everything possible was labelled so that she wasn't confused by any awkward questions. Fortunately though, most of the examiners were so impressed by all the extra work this involved, that they rarely failed her. The following day after starting Brownies Rachel really did seem unwell so I kept her home and took her to the GP for a check-up. As he said there was nothing wrong, we assumed it was just a reaction to all the emotion the day before. Alas, Rachel enjoyed her day off so much that she didn't want to return to school the next day, so once again I had to resort to dragging her there sobbing all the way.

On arrival I handed her over to her teacher who was quite sympathetic and made Rachel her special helper for the day. Whilst there, I made an appointment to see her teacher the next week to check how things were progressing after all our project work. Phil went with me that evening and we were pleased to see that her work had improved 100%. She was now consistently writing about half a page with only occasional reversals of letters, although her numbers were often reversed. I felt particularly pleased with this as I had done a lot of work with Rachel on letters in the holiday.

I had discovered that although she didn't respond to being shown or told how to do her letters, Rachel learnt quickly using tactile (touch) methods. We had therefore encouraged her to write letters all over the place using her pointing finger in sand, on the carpet, embossed wallpaper and even played games of guessing what was being written on our backs. We also used plasticine to make the letter shapes and when I felt she had conquered this, we moved onto rainbow writing, which involved writing a letter on top of itself in as many different colours as possible to create a rainbow image of each letter. The fact that her letters were now correct and we'd worked solely on them but not numbers, seemed to prove that our project had been successful. Consequently, I decided to work on numbers in the same way in the next holiday. Rachel's pictures had also improved and she'd made a good attempt at drawing a piano, an owl and a castle. She'd also made three cards with the pictures on the front instead of her usual style of pictures on the back. Altogether she was a different child; more relaxed, happy and confident, which was no doubt helped by the fact that she could now ride her bicycle as well. This change in Rachel was noticed and remarked upon by several different people.

Chapter Five

Projects and Problems

During the next half term holiday, I decided to do something about improving Rachel's concepts and logical thinking so borrowed some wooden association plaques from the Unit, where I worked, for this purpose. Although Rachel was keen to play with them, she really had no idea how to use them. They felt good to hold and were attractively painted, being designed rather like dominoes. However, the idea was not to match them but to put together two pictures with some association to each other; this could be two pieces of fruit, two things the same colour, both having wheels or even the same background colour. It could be played as simply or as cleverly as wished but my idea was to try and stretch her vocabulary and get her thinking more logically when trying to explain something. At first the game seemed little more than hard work; she knew she had to look for clues but failed to see even the obvious. Not only that, I was horrified to discover just how limited her vocabulary was. I was shocked to realise, by playing the game, that although she knew words like bed and table, she didn't know the word furniture, likewise with apple and banana but she didn't know that they were both fruits. This seemed to be the same for most group nouns but with other things like flowers or birds she knew the group noun but not their individual names like daisy, bluebell, parrot or peacock. Fortunately, she liked playing with the plaques and as I always found, it was amazing how quickly she improved in such situations.

We also did our planned work on her reversal of numbers to see if we could achieve the same level of success as we'd had with the letters. Although I was disappointed to see that she still did occasionally produce some letter reversals, I was pleased that this was nowhere near as bad as it had been originally. Now when I talk about working with Rachel or projects, it simply meant that we worked in a structured, step by step way for about 30 minutes after breakfast on whatever we were trying to achieve. To keep this fair, I always offered Gary the same individual time doing whatever he wanted, a fun scientific experiment or similar project or whatever he preferred. The rest of the day was spent normally, although if I found myself alone with Rachel, I did try to engage her in some constructive play during the afternoon while Gary was playing outside or elsewhere with friends. By surreptitiously providing the right materials we also tried improving her confidence in tracing and colouring as well but we really hoped that the weather would improve to allow us to try and get her into the water. As the school had its own swimming pool, I knew that swimming would start next half term but so far Rachel would only tolerate water ankle deep, after which she 'froze' and screamed with true terror. Unfortunately, that Whitsun, not only was the weather too cold for swimming or visiting the beach, the 1979 petrol shortage prevented us from driving to the nearest indoor pool.

On returning to school I was delighted to find that all our holiday work had paid off once more. Her general schoolwork was improving including her drawings and writing of numbers and she could now initiate conversations. Her language was still muddled at times but the temper tantrums were lessening, she appeared to be more confident and thankfully less dependent on me. Another improvement was in the way she played. For one thing she was beginning to play with children of normal ability and nearer her own age rather than with younger or slow learning children, she was also able to play alone for the first time and was enjoying games that involved rules rather than just act out a 'Mummies and Babies' type game.

Our next problem was when Gary began piano lessons as Rachel expected to have them too. We explained that she was younger and of course we knew she wasn't ready for them either. Even so every day after Gary had finished practicing, she insisted on trying to copy him until in the end we discussed the situation with the piano teacher, rather hoping that she would make the negative decision for us. Instead she said that as Rachel now had a good enough reading age at school, despite everything else, she was willing to try teaching her. Of course, Rachel was delighted with this verdict so we agreed to go along with it as long as everyone was happy. After all, I supposed it would help reinforce her left and right concepts and help to broaden her horizons if nothing else. Still, I did wonder how on earth her teacher would cope as I didn't think Rachel could discriminate between notes going up and down either aurally or visually in music.

That June we finally managed to get Rachel to willingly enter the sea, albeit only knee deep. Although I was pleased with this achievement, I was aware that she would have to go deeper than this in the school pool but thankfully that hadn't started yet. As Rachel was no better in the public swimming pools, preferring to stay in the paddling pool and screaming if we ever tried to take her into the shallow end of the large pool, we chose to save our money and stay on the beach, especially as she had grown up with this and it was less than a mile from our home. At least she would now play on the sand so one good thing to come from these trips was that she did at last, learn to catch a large beach ball when it was thrown to her from close range. Eventually, after many trips and inexhaustible patience (although I must admit mine did come close to being exhausted at times) we managed to get her into the water waist deep although her body was closely wrapped around mine and she was clinging on like a limpet for grim death! She clearly didn't like it but as she tolerated it, we felt that was enough; I could now leave the rest for the school to deal with. We did manage to enjoy a gentle splashing game while knee deep but again, she clung very firmly onto my hand. I also noticed that, when walking out of the water, she refused to walk anywhere near the seaweed and for some reason or other she was convinced that all the boats would overturn and all the people would drown! Was there no end to this girl's fears?

Well her first day for swimming lessons at school arrived and although she went off happily enough that day, the previous evening had been terrible! Her language was very confused and she was unable to ask me if Daddy had mended the puncture in her bicycle tyre. She ended up having a terrible tantrum, lying on the floor, hammering her heels and fists into the carpet and sobbing inconsolably. This went on for about 20 minutes until I could calm her enough to sit down quietly and try to sort out exactly what she wanted to say. This was the first tantrum for ages but unfortunately it wasn't to be the last. We then had word swapping all evening and she was unable to do her nightly reading from her school book although she tried as usual when Gary did his. She read lots of words in reverse like 'on' for 'no,' swapped around the order of the words in the sentence and even read the lines in the wrong order.

Her language continued to be her main problem and we had many similar episodes of frustration leading to temper tantrums that could last up to half an hour when she couldn't explain things or ask us what was important to her. Even a simple statement like "Dancing is at 6 o'clock" proved too difficult for her one day so we had all the usual heart-rending sobbing and thrashing about until she managed to say, *"Dancing is in half a - um - um - clock - you know - on the six."* Sadly, but admirably, Rachel never gave up or settled for second best or near enough. Consequently, her frustration always continued until we'd managed to establish exactly what she meant.

Sometimes Rachel wasn't really aware of her speech errors so, as long as we understood what she meant life continued peacefully, like the time she came up to me with both hands behind her back and instead of asking Which hand is the brown crayon in? She said, *"What colour is brown?"* Luckily, I guessed correctly and the incident passed by unnoticed by Rachel but we weren't always as blessed. Another difficulty that occurred due to her lack of understanding was when her grandparents were going to Ireland for a holiday. Rachel knew that they were going by boat so as usual, had little faith in their ability to stay afloat! She seemed convinced that even if the boat somehow miraculously succeeded in getting them there, they wouldn't be able to return home! I don't know to what primitive pagan country she thought they were visiting but it all seemed to be beyond her comprehension. I spent hours with her using a globe, drawing pictures and crossing off the days on a specially made calendar until they returned, bringing many small gifts for her and her brother. I think she developed some understanding of the situation in the end but it had certainly been a stressful time for her.

Although Rachel still used word substitutes and muddled words like 'undo' and 'do up,' it was obvious to us that she was trying hard to understand things now, although I think that is what led to her increased frustration tantrums. We also noticed that although she would query what a word meant when she saw or heard one she didn't remember, she never tried to use it herself afterwards. Remarkably, her reading age was now considered to be very good despite her occasional reversing of words, changing the word order or even missing out lines. Nonetheless, if we asked her a question about what she'd just read she could rarely explain the story or meaning of the text. Therefore, she was doing what is generally referred to as 'barking at print!' All in all though, despite her teacher reporting that she still needed a lot of individual attention, we could see that some progress had been made that term for which we were extremely thankful.

Rachel's main problems continued to be her poor use of vocabulary and her total inability to understand any intellectual conversations no matter how simply they were presented to her. She was the complete opposite of her brother Gary who soaked up information like a sponge. Yet, with the experience I'd gained from teaching the deaf children I felt I should have been able to get through to her better than I did. She could hold a gentle conversation with us, asking some questions and even answer a simple question in a one to one' situation but otherwise she appeared to just let things go completely 'over her head' unless she was physically involved.

By the end of June Rachel was becoming a much more affectionate child. I remember one day when she saw my mother walking up the road to our house for a visit, Rachel spontaneously ran up to her to give her a hug, which surprised my mother into saying, *"She's quite nice now isn't she?"* Now my mother was a very dutiful person who loved all her grandchildren equally and although I'm sure she would have bitten off her tongue had she realised what she inferred by that statement, I knew exactly what she meant. Thankfully Rachel was also becoming much happier and more confident and although her fears were still present, they were diminishing. She was also now beginning to cope with and enjoy playing simple games with us like Snap or Snakes and Ladders and thank goodness she didn't seem to need our constant company any more.

Chapter Six
Let Battle Commence

Eventually we were told that the Educational Psychologist, Kevin Brown, would be able to see Rachel in school on 5th July 1979, after which he would do a home visit to discuss the results with us. Coincidentally though, it was Rachel's Open Evening at school the day before Kevin's assessment. All day at work I was feeling apprehensive about how the school staff would act towards us regarding the pending investigation, knowing that we had been the ones to instigate this. So far there had been no response from them whilst waiting for it to arrive, so I hoped that they would continue in the same vein, although instinctively I expected to face some reaction that evening. Julie reassured me during our lunch time chat, that they could do absolutely nothing to stop the assessment and told me that if any comments were made against it, we could reply that we 'knew our parental rights and that was what we wanted'.

On arriving home from work we both washed and changed to present ourselves in our best light, in spite of the fact that they had seen one or both of us twice a day ever since Rachel had started at the school. On the way there I explained to Phil what Julie had said but it seemed that he wasn't as bothered about their opinion as much as me and already felt that way. Nevertheless, he did admit that it was nice to know we would be safe in saying such a thing in defence of our actions should the need arise.

On examination of her work all our opinions about her improvement were confirmed. Her reading age was high even if she was 'barking at print,' her written work was much better with only occasional reversals of letters and she had achieved a good enough standard in maths. Her pictures were much improved generally in as much as the people had gained more details like arms and hands but she still really concentrated on drawing houses, trees and flowers whenever possible. Her teacher was a kindly Scots lady who did her best to support Rachel in class but proceeded to tell us not to worry about her as she felt Rachel just lacked confidence and simply needed reassurance. Well I had spent the last 7 years telling Rachel that being nice was much more I important than being clever but so far, it'd had little effect. We said nothing to this comment but were surprised when she went on to say that the Headteacher had asked to see us before we went home. We therefore proceeded immediately to the Head's inner sanctum feeling somewhat like lambs going to the slaughter but with Phil reminding me that there was nothing to be worried about. They couldn't stop us and it may even be about something else. However, it transpired that all my feelings of apprehension had been justified after all and I was more than grateful for Julie's advice and support. Her phrase about 'We know our parental rights' kept floating about in my head whilst the Head sat there telling us that she felt Rachel just needed more confidence.

We politely listened but I was shocked to hear her say that Rachel could be inhibited by our expectations! We tried to discuss things with the Head saying that we knew Rachel was a nervous child but denied asking too much from her. We explained that we had always told her that she could only do her best and not to worry about what she scored. Instead we had always reassured her that we would help her overcome anything that worried her should her teachers want more. I described how Rachel had always been in awe of her brother and could be inhibited by his achievements as she used to get upset when he could read and she couldn't although that was now in the past and explained that Rachel herself was a perfectionist who set herself high standards. If Rachel wanted to show us something like a handstand we would watch and dutifully admire the performance but if she knew she could do better she would not accept our praise but insist on trying again until she was satisfied that she had shown us her best effort! I tried to explain all this to the Head and offered to send in my diary, that I had kept on Rachel since she was 4 years old, for her to read but it was obvious that she had already formed her opinion and was only intent on persuading us to cancel the appointment next day. In fact, she told us that Kevin's time would be better spent seeing another child that they wanted assessed as he was more disruptive in school! When she had finished, we quietly quoted our prepared phrase about parental rights. I also remember telling her that should we be proven wrong we would apologise but if we were right, I would expect an apology from her but I don't think she answered.

On the way home I started doubting myself again and wishing that I had been blessed with Phil's quiet confidence in his own opinions. How could all those professionals not see Rachel as we did? Surely they couldn't all be wrong? Admittedly she was a 'highly-strung' child to say the least; maybe they were right after all. Even so, if it was all caused by a lack of confidence I wanted to know why. Why was she so frightened of everything? I didn't believe in the Head's theory that we inhibited her. Instead, I wondered if we were the only ones, in whom she had enough confidence to show her true self, complete with all her demonstrations of despair and frustration! Instinctively I felt that it had something to do with Rachel's understanding. I felt sure she had some sort of language problem because once we'd managed to make her understand something, the problems surrounding that precise situation gradually disappeared. I was so glad that Kevin would be seeing her the next day and hoped that it wouldn't be too long before he came to discuss the results with us.

The next day I sent the diary into school with Rachel as promised, albeit some badly written, emotional notes in a scrappy old notebook discarded by one of the children, but I didn't care as I felt the end justified the means. Nevertheless, I was amazed at the letter I received with its return that afternoon. I really don't know why, I can only think it was due to my shock and indignation, but I kept that letter for many years afterwards. It simply said:
'Thank you for the notebook herewith returned.' She then said that she had seen Rachel that morning to explain that Mr Brown would be seeing some children that afternoon and she had been chosen to be one of them. Didn't she trust me to explain such things to my own child?! She went on to say that she had given Rachel a Preliminary Test, which I thought was outrageous and totally unfair on Rachel. She also had the gall to tell me that during her chat Rachel had been able to explain about her grandparents' holiday in Ireland and of their present to her of a charm for her bracelet. According to her, Rachel had understood what was expected of her and had replied quickly throughout the test. I felt extremely angry and indignant about the whole episode. Not only about subjecting a child to such a session, including another test, knowing that they were to shortly undergo intensive and important investigations but because the Head had no idea of the abnormal amount of teaching Rachel had required in order to understand about her grandparent's holiday. Not only that, Rachel had, obviously forgotten about all the other little presents she had received apart from the charm! By the time I had read the last paragraph I was completely incensed.

In this she concluded that 'Rachel did not produce the symptoms of stress that we observed because she was relaxed and at ease at school.' She even suggested that we 'could be unconsciously expecting Rachel to get muddled so she did - much as if one visits an austere Aunt who expects you to drop one of her best glasses - so you do!' She finished by telling us that Rachel had been seen by Mr Brown who would be in touch with us.

I really couldn't believe that I had received such a letter from a professional person and thanked God that Kevin had assessed her that day. Although Phil was equally as furious at the tone of the letter, he felt that as Rachel had received the assessment we wanted, it was now best to wait quietly for the result. He said that he felt we'd caused enough ripples, so didn't want to cause any more. Quite honestly, I don't think either of us could have written a reply to that letter. It didn't seem to deserve one!

Although it seemed like an eternity Kevin arranged to see us at home, one evening a week later. I cannot explain the feelings of relief we felt whilst talking to him as it became apparent that he not only understood everything we were trying to say but that he also agreed with us, that Rachel did have severe specific learning difficulties. He also said that she behaved as he'd expect for a child born as she was in such a hurry. He wasn't surprised that she saw fear in everything and told us that with her anxiety and degree of problems he was surprised that she wasn't worse than she was. He even congratulated us on how we had handled her!

This was the first professional to acknowledge our problems, apart from Julie, and not criticise our methods of coping with them. He said that he could see that Rachel had suffered from poor motor control (co-ordination) and spatial awareness (understanding the position of one thing and how it relates to something else in space), which were both important for reading and writing, but thanks to our help and her IQ she had achieved a reasonable standard for a 7 year old. Kevin also said that Rachel had a good IQ of about 120, which was such a relief after being told by so many other professionals that she wasn't as bright as we thought and that we were expecting too much from her We had been right to believe in her and fight her cause!

He explained that in some tests Rachel had scored as high as for an 8 ½ year old but had failed four of the five sections tested. He said that her problems included: poor motor control, spatial awareness and crossed laterality (a right-handed person should develop right-sided dominance but Rachel used either hand, foot or eye, which meant that her brain hadn't developed a dominant side.) She also had problems sequencing a series of items like pictures, numbers, letters or instructions and had trouble interpreting information even when presented visually. Kevin noted Rachel's extreme tension and determination to succeed at the highest possible level and said that without that determination her scores would have been a lot lower, given the degree of her problems. It was seeing that amount of effort that was needed all the time in order for her to keep up, even at a low level, that broke my heart and I was so glad that he had acknowledged this.

Kevin finished his visit by offering to see Rachel on a weekly basis to help relieve her tension, try to improve her confidence and discover any other underlying cause for all her abnormal fears. At the same time, he would guide us through a remedial programme of activities, recommend some suitable play materials available from the Toy Library and some work books that would be useful for us to use at home. I asked Kevin about my theory that Rachel might have a language problem but he said he wasn't sure. He said that as she had such gross learning difficulties, he recommended getting rid of them first and see what we are left with.

I recalled Julie saying that if Rachel had a language disorder, she thought that Kevin would notice it so, at that time, this seemed a reasonable suggestion and we were glad to accept the advice and support of the first person to offer any real help apart from her. We soon fell into a routine of weekly sessions after school with Kevin, which Rachel enjoyed immensely. She idolised him and worked hard at everything he suggested, after which he would have a chat with either Phil or me, to see how Rachel had coped that week, when we went to collect her. Sometimes he even chatted to Gary, so in this way he supported us all as a family and guided us through the work books and activities that he'd recommended us to use at home.

Meanwhile, I read as many books as I could about Rachel's specific learning difficulties and how to help her overcome them, which I found both enlightening and fascinating. From these I learnt that the left and right patterning involved in crawling was important for stimulating the areas of never crawled but had been a 'bum-shuffler' instead. Furthermore, when we checked this out with her, she actually found it quite difficult to learn to crawl. We also began looking out for any toys that would help with her sequencing problems and bought her a kaleidoscope in an attempt to encourage right eye dominance. In order to fit in Kevin's recommended half hour homework, we found it best to do them as soon as seemed reasonable, after her drink and biscuit on arriving home from school, while she was still geared up for work. Meanwhile Gary would do his school homework or play. Regrettably though, this meant that Phil often came home from work to find me sitting down at the table working with Rachel or quietly trying to explain something to her. Fortunately, on these days he was quite happy to cook the evening meal, saying that he preferred the role of chef to being Rachel's tutor, so thankfully we all slotted comfortably into our niches.

To wait until after the evening meal for these work sessions would have been impossible due to all the children's activities such as Brownies,

Cubs, dancing (which was important in helping both her awareness of left and right and her sequencing problems), gymnastics and performing in the local productions. We seriously wondered if we should stop some of these hobbies as they were becoming hard to fit into an already tight schedule but quite honestly this was where Rachel was able to relax and excel away from school. Not only that, we felt that a lot of her hobbies were helping her both remedially as well as boosting her self-respect and confidence. However, Rachel worked extremely hard to keep up her quota of Brownie badges and practiced morning, noon and night to learn her dance routines. One girl who stayed with us for 18 months and subsequently became a family friend can well remember Rachel practicing her tap routines on the kitchen floor before leaving for school each morning. She said she found it more effective than her alarm clock!

Chapter Seven
Confusion, Fears and Phobias

That Summer we continued to spend 30 minutes a day working in Kevin's workbooks but otherwise just relaxed and enjoyed the holiday. It was good to see the gradual improvement in Rachel's fine motor skills although she still couldn't write on lines. I was aware that this would soon be expected of her in Junior school but wasn't bothered, as I knew there would be plenty of others just the same and that there were more important things to work on first. I still believed that Rachel's language was her biggest problem, which in turn led to a lack of understanding that ultimately caused her an amazing list of fears and phobias. I was convinced that this lack of language was the crux of the whole matter but everyone else seemed to think that she was OK, just shy and not as bright as we thought she was! Despite having her IQ confirmed at 120!

Although she was beginning to improve in her conversational skills and take an intelligent interest in some things, I was still concerned about the way she still muddled her words. One day she wanted to ask for shepherd's pie for dinner but just couldn't make me understand what she wanted for a long time. This resulted in another lengthy tantrum lasting a good twenty minutes until finally, by a process of elimination, I was able to guess what she meant. She began by saying, *"Can we have um, um, um - something for dinner - you know"* She tried to explain but just got confused and more and more frustrated. *"Potatoes with little bits in"* was tried so I showed her some potato salad with chives that was in the fridge thinking I'd got it at last. No, that wasn't it, she meant *"meat with little bits in."* Now I knew she loved salami so I took that out of the fridge to show her. Finally, after much sobbing and thrashing about until we were both exhausted emotionally if not physically, we established that she wanted, *"little bits of meat with potato on top!"* She was 7 years old but still couldn't ask for what was one of her favourite meals. I really don't know who hurt the most.

Another similar episode evolved around food again. Phil was going out but, unknown to me, he had told Rachel that he would bring back some fancy cakes for tea as a treat. She was obviously delighted with this so wanted to share the information with me but failed completely to convey the message. I thought she was asking if Daddy would bring something back but, as I knew he wasn't going to collect anything, I simply kept explaining that *"No, he isn't bringing anything back."* Understandably this distressed her very much as she was looking forward to the cakes but I just couldn't fathom out what the problem was until Phil returned bearing his gift of fancy cakes for tea!

One of the biggest things Rachel had to cope with that summer was the unexpected arrival of our Swedish pen friends, which completely disrupted any plans that we had previously made. I hadn't realised before just how much I had explained everything to Rachel about any family plans for such things as excursions, which of course we always carried out, unless prevented by an emergency or some such event. Now here we were suddenly following another family's plans that seemed to be constantly changing. Our week was completely turned upside down and although everyone else enjoyed it, Rachel seemed to find it very hard to cope with. It meant that I couldn't prepare her adequately for anything in advance because even when I explained the plan to her, to ensure that she understood, the programme was often changed due to the weather or because we had run out of time. Consequently, Rachel felt confused, insecure and frustrated. We also seemed to spend a lot of time on the beach with our guests and although she now tolerated the sand and sea she still could not go anywhere near the seaweed. Neither would she walk on the pier as it was made from planks of wood that didn't quite meet, so the sea could be glimpsed beneath. Rachel was so frightened by this that she cried and clung to us even when being carried over it, while her fear of boats seemed to be becoming more of an obsession rather like her fear of motor bikes.

Later that month when Gary went to Cub camp Rachel felt worried and insecure all the time he was away. Even when we went to visit his camp site, she 'froze' at the entrance and had to be carried in. Yet again she was afraid of another unknown place until she was able to accept that it seemed to be reasonably safe and was able to relax enough to enjoy the visit. Personally, I began to appreciate that we could never really prepare Rachel for anything by giving her explanations as she only really understood by experiencing it for herself.

While in the area we chose to visit a nearby large tank museum that Phil was keen to see but once again, Rachel didn't want to go as she couldn't absorb the information that we were trying to give her. She knew that tanks were big and that soldiers had used them for fighting so she was terrified to go and see them. Evidently, she believed they might move or maybe even start firing and no amount of reassurance would convince her that they were secured to the spot and not able to work in that setting. Yet again, we had to carry her into the museum where she initially refused to explore with the other children. Gradually she accepted that everything seemed to be safe and that nothing untoward had happened when other people climbed on the tanks, until eventually she plucked up enough courage to sit in one herself. By the end of the day we were even able to explain to her a little about their use in the war and she showed an intelligent curiosity. It was fantastic to see her being interested and responsive.

At times like this I wondered if we were being cruel to Rachel when we pushed her into such situations but I always came away feeling that we had done the right thing by overcoming yet another obstacle. I was afraid that if we let her fears govern her life, she would not only miss out on a lot of fun but also develop into a nervous wreck. I was convinced that if I could only teach her that most things were under control, she would have more confidence in the world. It was just a matter of finding the right key to enable us to unlock her mind and help her to comprehend.

As previously said, she wouldn't go anywhere with close friends or even family unless either Phil, Gary or I were with her. Even so there were still times when she became upset, like the time we visited a local zoo and she flatly refused to enter a dimly lit tunnel. She reacted by doing her usual trick of 'freezing' on the spot, making herself ramrod stiff and becoming very difficult to carry; although by now I think Phil was becoming quite an expert at this. Another day a family friend took Gary and her bowling but despite appearing to have coped quite well with this, her behaviour on returning home that evening was diabolical. She was swearing, shouting, angry, moody and upset about anything and everything although we couldn't understand why. We simply put her to bed and hoped for peace the following morning.

Rachel was also genuinely worried about her brother's health as he frequently suffered from ear infections, large lumps and bumps on his forehead and even concussion a few times, due to bruising of the brain, owing to his undiagnosed Haemophilia. One day when he had a bad cut on the back of his head at school, Rachel confided in me that she was afraid he might die because he had lost a lot of blood, although the whole incident had been far more dramatic than serious. As Rachel saw danger in everything, she continued to be over-protective towards her cousin Brett, while her eating habits still remained a problem, although they were inclined to be inconsistent. I therefore wondered if this was a form of manipulative behaviour being used for effect, like her apparent 'hypochondria.' She either had a very low pain threshold or was using yet another attention seeking tactic.

Even though she enjoyed visiting the theatre Rachel always had mixed feelings about the cinema because, in those days, we nearly always entered into a darkened room. She also found the climax of the film, both in the cinema and at home on TV, upsetting so rarely watched television and had to be thoroughly reassured that any visit to the cinema would not be too traumatic, before agreeing to come with us.

Another problem with Rachel due to her lack of language, was her poor memory. We had often taken the children on day trips to London for various reasons, which Gary always enjoyed, absorbing all the history and busy atmosphere but unless we had living proof to prompt her memory, Rachel always seemed to forget about it soon afterwards, which was very frustrating. As Rachel was adamant that she had never been to London and seemed to have no comprehension of its importance to England, we decided to dedicate a week for daytrips, 'doing the sights' and ensuring that she had her photograph taken at as many places as we could manage. We also chose to use slides so that we could make a bigger impact when showing them to her at regular intervals afterwards. We went to a lot of trouble preparing her for these visits by using simple but well-illustrated children's guide books, to ensure that she understood as much as possible.

Consequently Buckingham Palace, the Coronation Coach and Number 10 Downing Street all meant something to her for the first time and we were rewarded by her questions and interest on the trips. Despite all this I don't think we entirely succeeded though, as when we arrived at Buckingham Palace Rachel was convinced that the Queen was sure to invite us in for a cup of tea when she saw us there! However, she was not daunted when this failed to happen so, on arrival at 10 Downing Street, she was adamant that the Prime Minister would definitely ask us inside for some refreshment. Phil and I had spent several weeks talking about the proposed expeditions and  what each day would cover. We both thought we should include a ride on the London underground tube train one day for Gary and that we would try to conquer Rachel's fear of boats, once and for all, by incorporating a river trip from Westminster to Greenwich on another day. Not surprisingly, once Rachel knew of both these plans, she became extremely difficult to live with.

We needed incredible patience for about a couple of weeks prior to these outings, especially over the last 2 days preceding the events. Moreover, her behaviour became impossible and she 'froze' at the actual time but any less preparation would have led to near hysteria. The day before the river trip Rachel was tense and irritable because of her fear of boats and she stayed close beside me all the time. I just gritted my teeth and tried to carry on as normal but it was far from easy. Thankfully though all our tactics paid off as she successfully survived the journey up the river, after which we all had a pleasant day. The tube also required the same amount of reassurance with her being carried on board but of course this passed by quickly without too much trauma involved.

Her final fear that summer concerned her pending transfer into Junior School. Rachel was quite familiar with the actual building, staff and numbers of children because Gary was already attending there but she was now having fears about having to write stories. She was obviously very worried about this and I knew it would be impossible for her to write more than the usual few lines but I presumed we would just have to cope with each step as it came along. I therefore hoped that she would have a sympathetic teacher or that Kevin Brown would be able to help in some way.

Chapter Eight
Is Help on the Way?

In spite of all her apprehension Rachel seemed to 'sail' into Junior School without any problems at all. This may have been an improvement on her part or could have been due to her familiarity with the campus, which must have paid untold dividends. She was also lucky enough to have Gary's previous teacher whom she knew plus the unexpected transfer of one of her infant teachers to the junior staff, making another familiar face to whom she could relate. We knew that Gary's presence in the school was her biggest support though, which was proven one day when he stayed home with another ear infection and Rachel refused to go without him. Although she did go under protest it was obvious that she felt insecure knowing that he wouldn't be around all day, even though they would have been in different classrooms.

As the term progressed her mood began to change as Gary was doing well, gaining lots of team points as merit awards and had become a free reader. Regrettably, this made Rachel feel very inferior as all her efforts, which were immense, were going by unacknowledged. Consequently, Rachel began saying that she didn't like school as she was afraid of being told off and one day, I had to collect her at lunchtime as she claimed to feel unwell. However, she was perfectly all right once she got home! Nevertheless, we were quite pleased with the way she had coped with the major transition from Infant to Junior School, along with her general improvement and the fact that she was now beginning to reveal her thoughts to us.

Her school reports always said the same thing for every subject; good effort but slow and academically immature, although some progress had been made. At the next Open Evening we were pleased to learn that Rachel was able to start on the Junior reading scheme and her hand writing was much improved although still not on the line. Nonetheless, as she wanted to run before she could walk as usual, she was upset because everyone else was starting to do 'joined up writing!' However, her main problem now seemed to be coping with tens and units, which we resolved to work on in the next holiday. Although we had all liked her teacher in the past and thought we'd established a good rapport, I'm afraid this was no longer the case now that she had Rachel to teach instead of Gary. In fact, she told us in no uncertain terms, that it was a pity that we had ever seen Kevin Brown and that we were pushing Rachel to try and achieve what was beyond her capabilities. I tried explaining that we were in fact doing just the opposite as, apart from Kevin Brown's books, all our activities and been based on basic infant reception work, in order to establish the simple patterning needed to write letters and numbers. I also explained that we felt this had been successful as it had always been followed by an improvement in the specific area on which we'd worked, but she just dismissed this by saying that it must have been pure coincidence each time. When I asked what she would have done to help her child that she was dragging to school daily, sobbing because she couldn't cope, she didn't answer - but I later found out that she was in fact pregnant with her first child. I couldn't help wondering how much she could actually relate to our situation but I knew for certain that she didn't approve of us helping Rachel or involving Kevin Brown.

That autumn Rachel 'bravadoed' herself into attending a Hallowe'en party and was even more pleased with herself when she won first prize as a witch. She was also more at ease at the Bonfire parties that year, even allowing herself to wander away from us a little at a time. Sadly, this newly found confidence and self-respect was soon to take a great knock when the game of 'jacks' became the latest craze. Rachel had already said that she wanted some for Christmas so we decided to leave it until then, knowing how difficult this would be for her to cope with. The game consisted of throwing a very small ball into the air and catching it with one hand whilst simultaneously picking up one or more of the five small metal objects called jacks. We knew that as Rachel still had trouble catching a larger ball with two hands, she would not find it easy to cope with everything that jacks involved. For a couple of days Rachel became very difficult and hard to live with but finally revealed that no one would let her play jacks with them at school because she was "*silly and stupid at it.*" She was particularly hurt when her best friend also refused to let her join in the game. The next morning this all came to a head when she sobbed and messed about instead of getting herself ready for school. Her behaviour became quite out of hand as she resorted to her ridiculously stupid behaviour that she'd used when younger to avoid conversations. I really didn't know what to do to pacify her so let her carry promised to buy her some jacks the same day and of course something equivalent for Gary. That afternoon after school, she only took about two steps inside the front door when she sat down on the floor with her coat still on to open the packet and tried to play the game. Of course, she couldn't catch the ball with two hands let alone one, which led to the inevitable frustration, followed by a lot of temper at times and occasional outbursts of tears but thankfully no tantrums. It nearly broke my heart knowing how hurt she was whilst being totally unable to help her. All I could do was watch her desperate attempts to catch that wretched ball and let her work it through for herself. I think it was one of the hardest things I had ever done. She hardly moved from the spot all evening, continuously trying to catch that elusive ball. The next morning, she practiced again before school and again in the evening, using every spare minute she could between coming home from school until bedtime. She really pushed herself and absolutely nothing else was allowed to take precedence. It took all my strength to help her cope but I found it very hard to keep my temper with all her ridiculously childish behaviour that accompanied her efforts. Eventually after nearly a week of intense practice, she felt competent enough to take her own jacks into school to play with, alongside her friends. Even though she had not become an accomplished player she could at least keep up with the peer group pressure of owning and appearing to play jacks.

As Christmas brought its usual amount of excitement into the household it also led Rachel into her usual regression of muddled words, frustration and tantrums but on the whole we all coped quite well. One day Rachel wanted to ask me what her zodiacal birth sign was but as this came completely 'out of the blue' I had no idea what she meant when she came up to me and asked *"What's my name?"* Well I knew she was confused but I didn't think she was that bad but irrespectively I gave the obvious answer and said, *"Rachel."* *"No, what am I?"* she persisted. *"A girl,"* I replied getting equally as confused and frustrated by the conversation. Eventually, by a process of elimination and playing 20 questions we were able to decode her question and establish that her star sign was Aries, much to her satisfaction and our relief,

There were still some reversals in her writing but the bonus of that holiday was that she learnt to catch a ball properly. She even managed to catch it one handed when thrown to her from a distance of about 4 metres (just over

4 yards) and to catch balls that were bounced to her. That Christmas we gave Rachel a watch with the words half, quarter and past written on it as well as the usual numbers, as these were the days before digital clocks and watches, in the hope that it would help her.

For our work on tens and units Phil made a hundred cubes each of 1 centimetre (cm) dimension to represent units; and ten rods; each measuring 10cm by 1cm to represent the tens. Therefore, by laying down 10 cubes alongside a rod she could see that 10 units were the same as one ten. These worked so successfully that she was able to use them whenever she had any tens and units homework. For addition she religiously counted out all the necessary cubes for the units and then swapped them over in groups of tens for a rod, until she could see how many units were left to write in the answer box. She would then count up her tens rods including any that she had transferred over from the units and consequently got the right answer. I don't think she entirely understood the concept for some time, as she certainly needed to use the cubes and rods as a prop for a very long time, but the tension was eased and she began to get more ticks in her maths book. No doubt her teacher thought this was yet another coincidence but we were happy that she had crossed another hurdle.

Although Rachel was making steady progress in most areas albeit a long way behind her peers, her piano teacher told us what we had expected to hear a lot earlier. Although Rachel had coped initially, she was now making no further progress, so the teacher thought it best to stop the lessons. I hated telling Rachel and felt guilty for having let her try in the first place when I saw how devastated she was. I had hoped that Rachel would have come to the same conclusion herself first but far from it, she was still just as determined to be as good as her friends.

At times of despair like this I used to think Rachel might have been happier in a different family or environment, where she wouldn't have been surrounded by lots of people succeeding in so many different areas, but in my heart, I knew that we had to carry on supporting her and teaching her ourselves in the only way we knew how, which was basically by following our gut instincts. Even so, when Rachel told us that she wanted to learn the recorder if she couldn't learn the piano, my heart sank and plummeted to the bottom of my boots! I honestly didn't think she could manage, as one reason she'd had to give up piano was because she couldn't distinguish whether the notes were going up or down the stave on the music, and I was sure she wouldn't manage in the recorder group at school. I therefore initially ignored her requests to pursue the recorder until one day she found my old descant recorder under a pile of music. She immediately sat on the stairs and began to subject us to all the usual horrible squeaks and squeals that most parents of recorder enthusiasts have experienced at one time or another. There was nothing for it but to appease her by trying to get a proper note out of the thing. It took me ages to succeed, after which she wanted to learn more. I showed her a simple scale of three notes using three fingers and a thumb and hoped that this would satisfy her until she became bored but as usual, she just kept on pestering us to let her join the recorder club at school.

I really knew that she wouldn't cope with another failure so soon and I certainly wasn't ready for it at all. Kevin Brown also agreed with us that the recorder group would be too difficult for her but Rachel would not accept this. It was then that I had a brain-wave and went to see a neighbour who lived a couple of doors along our road. Her husband was a Baptist Minister and an organ enthusiast, having made a few records. In fact, the whole family, including their three daughters were all very musical. I also knew that this, kind and gentle, lady helped out on frequent occasions in the music department at Rachel's school; including running the recorder groups.

I therefore decided to explain the whole situation to her and asked if she thought she could help Rachel by giving her some private, simplified recorder lessons at home and at her own pace, until she was either able to join a suitable group or she became bored enough to give up herself. To my immense relief and gratitude, she agreed to help, so Rachel began her private, weekly recorder lessons after school, which proved amazingly successful. This compassionate lady managed to find a super music book that used an extremely simple layout, with large notes printed on the lines. Each page moved the pupil on in easy stages and must have been designed for young infants but Rachel didn't care as she was happy to be learning music again. Amazingly, this scheme proved so successful that Rachel eventually, Rachel was able to join a group run by the same person at school.

Her first year in Junior School continued more or less uneventfully with only a few minor hiccups like the time the Headmaster 'phoned to say that that we were wasting our money buying Rachel school dinners, as she was persistently taking the minimum allowed and leaving the maximum amount accepted. He therefore suggested that Rachel had packed lunches and not be allowed to throw anything away at school so that way we could monitor the amount she ate ourselves. The next time I had a 'phone call from the school was to tell me to meet them at the local Minor Injuries Unit as Rachel had broken a school rule by running in the classroom. Consequently, she had slipped, banged her head on the side of a desk and cut her ear which needed three stitches. Subsequently, Rachel was in such a state of shock that she coped remarkably well but when she went back for their removal, she was so scared, the poor girl couldn't even cry. Instead she just sat there shaking like a leaf and whimpering like a lost puppy. She looked really pathetic but I was proud of the way she coped as she was no worse for the Doctor to handle than any other child would have been. It was some time later when Rachel told me that she wasn't actually running in the classroom but skipping back to her seat because she was so happy. She had just been given her very first merit mark for effort!

Rachel also coped well with the school swimming lessons in as much as we didn't have any scenes although she made little progress as she was still too tense in the water. As every child took part in the end of term swimming gala, Rachel was only in the walking race along with all the other non-swimmers but we were just glad that she was able to enjoy the event as this was a big step forward for her in itself. She continued to work diligently through Kevin Brown's workbooks although they were beginning to become difficult for her. The tasks, designed to improve her fine motor skills and visual perception (understanding what she saw), were at just the right level but the part designed to improve her language and comprehension was too hard in places. Sometimes we would leave that section and go back to it some weeks later, which seemed to help.

By the time Rachel was 8 years old her language remained the hardest part to cope with. As she had no real concept of time, everything in the future was referred to as tomorrow while everything in the past would be yesterday, no matter how long ago. Still, we were now blessed with a word that most parents of toddlers dread hearing, *"Why?"* This was a new but well-voiced word in our vocabulary, along with her gradual desire to learn and improve her general knowledge. As this had been such a long awaited event we were thrilled and enjoyed the novelty of being able to explain things to her.

That summer Rachel chose to go with her Brownies on their annual pack holiday and we were delighted as she had refused to go previously. No doubt she felt more comfortable about the idea since we had camped as a family and had also helped at Gary's Cub camp after Phil had become a Cub Leader. Now, it seemed, she was ready to go off on her own for the first time and what a success it was! After her return from that pack holiday Rachel was noticeably far more mature and confident especially in social settings.

At the end of her first year in Juniors I had another 'phone call from the Headmaster to ask our opinion of Rachel and how we would feel about placing her in a class of twelve handpicked, slow learning children for her second year? Obviously, we welcomed the idea as we felt she not only needed more individual help but would be relieved of the pressure from all the peer group competition and trying to succeed beyond her capabilities. Personally though, I was intrigued that Rachel's class teacher, who'd previously tried to tell us that Rachel was no worse than many others, had actually recommended her for such a class but felt too relieved to pass any comment.

Rachel developed a great deal in that Remedial Class thanks to the teacher's special care and understanding. He was older than her previous teacher so came with a wealth of experience to share, whilst being blessed with enormous patience and genuine concern for each individual child's problem. Now that everything possible was being done at last for Rachel, Phil and I felt able to relax and accept the situation that she was just a slow learner who was making her own progress at her own speed. She would probably always be the same but I did hope that she would manage to reach a reasonable level, enough to cope with everyday life, even if a little late. Unfortunately, though, it seemed Rachel didn't feel the same way, as I was still constantly having to tell her that being nice was much more important than being clever. She initially loved the group and improved by happily taking part in all the activities and even began swimming with arm bands while in that class. However, towards the end of the year Rachel began to object to the group as other children in the school were beginning to call them names like 'baby' when they played with constructive toys, so we eventually talked to her teacher about this as it was becoming a real problem. We really didn't want anything to spoil what had been such a success as we knew both the teacher and special teaching had been exactly what she'd needed. He then surprised us by disclosing that Rachel wasn't really like the rest of the class. He said that most of the other children in his class were of low ability and indicated that some also had other social problems, apart from one child who was there to catch up on schoolwork as she'd missed a lot of schooling due to ill health, but he didn't feel that Rachel fitted into either of those categories. He acknowledged that despite all her difficulties Rachel presented as a bright child and quite understood her feelings about the class and the other children's teasing. He then went on to say that as Rachel had made sufficient progress to integrate into a normal class for three topic lessons a week, he would try to arrange this for the next term. This system worked extremely well as it gave a balance to Rachel's life in school; she had the support of the special class and teacher without the status of wholly belonging to the group. At the same time, she could enjoy the prestige of integration without suffering the continual pressure to succeed alongside her peers.

Unfortunately, Rachel was placed in normal classes for the third and fourth years with no extra support but she managed to struggle through at her own pace with no major setbacks. When she was 9 years old Kevin Brown felt he had reached the end of his therapy but promised to assess Rachel prior to her transfer into Senior School. I don't know why we didn't remind him then, that he had initially agreed to consider whether or not Rachel had in fact got a language problem at this stage, as we ourselves had repeatedly suspected. Sadly, Julie had moved to Dorset by now so was no longer available to discuss our dilemmas, whilst Rachel herself was making some steady progress in all areas both socially and at school.

Retrospectively, I think we could have been distracted by the fact that her brother had recently been diagnosed with Haemophilia, which certainly explained his previous bruising problems but this now manifested itself by causing multiple problems within his school due to a lot of basic ignorance and fear amongst the staff. Subsequently they were frightened of every minor injury that Gary encountered, resulting in him being hospitalised in

London at St Thomas' Hospital.

Meanwhile, Rachel's class teacher made an interesting observation at the end of her fourth year in Junior school when her class were doing a multiple-choice Richmond test paper. It was during this that he noticed Rachel using what he described as 'belt and braces' tactics by using the double security of checking everything twice over. He went on to describe how he had watched her repeatedly re-reading all the questions and answers offered, before attempting to choose her answer. So much so that she only completed a quarter of the paper in the allotted time but had in fact actually answered every question she'd attempted correctly. Therefore, although she'd scored 100% in the finished answers, her recorded mark was only 25% due to the amount completed.

Chapter Nine

Still More Struggles

When Rachel was 11 years old her brother spent a few months in a London hospital which of course involved a lot of family visiting. He was on a large children's ward that had an excellent Play Leader who inspired Rachel into thinking that this was an area of work that she might enjoy. She had always had a natural ability with children and had enjoyed the challenge of working with the children in the Unit for the Hearing Impaired where I worked but now, she realised for the first time that she might like to work with sick   children or those with disabilities in some way.

Rachel continued to develop socially and grew in confidence but she still needed a lot of our support to succeed. This became particularly apparent

when she went on Guide camp and her Guide Captain reported to us that she had overheard Rachel talking to herself one day when she was shut in a tent alone, unaware of anyone being outside to hear her. She was heard to say repeatedly that she *was* going to stay at camp and she *was* going to cope with everything! I don't think her leader had been so fully aware of Rachel's inner struggles until that moment but something similar was noticed on each subsequent camp even though she chose to go along each time herself. One of the things that Rachel found hard at Guides besides all the badge work, was being a Patrol Leader as she lacked the authority to lead and manage girls so near her own age, along with all their various teenage moods. I think she found this particularly frustrating as she was so good at dealing with younger children. Nevertheless, Rachel still managed to gain the Baden Powell Award which is the highest badge awarded to Guides and was proud to be the youngest person in her Company to achieve this. Dancing continued to be of great remedial benefit to Rachel, as well as a pleasure, but although she still needed extra lessons to learn the routines until she was nearly 15 years old. It wasn't until then that she was able to cope alone for the first time, with learning five new dances for a show in ballet, tap and modern alongside her peers at normal lessons. Although ballet was still her favourite subject, probably due to its classically structured discipline, she hated the improvisation that was part of this class as it required her to use imagination that she found so difficult.

It was about this time that Rachel began looking for a part time Saturday or holiday job. Although good with children she wasn't sure about doing straight-forward work as a Nanny, so tried for a shop assistant post instead but after one morning in a busy craft shop, she was told that she was too slow mentally for such work. Sometime later she managed to cope with a job in a small newsagent in one of the back streets of town where the pace was probably slower.

It was always in school that her biggest problems seemed to lie. Although Kevin Brown had assessed her as promised and said that he thought she would cope with Senior School, he then left the district and was replaced by a woman who was all but unavailable. Rachel did in fact cope initially, but only just and only by enormous efforts on her part, because it was against her nature to let herself fail if she could prevent it. It was this degree of determination to succeed, that gave us the strength and motivation to help her, although it was very demanding along with all the other household chores and commitments to family life, not to mention both our jobs. Although her reading and writing skills were now of a good enough standard, she still had occasional spelling problems and her sentence structure was often muddled and immature.

The half hour homework on a subject every night was taking her at least two hours to complete due to her slow thought processing, difficulty in understanding the task or text involved and her inability to decide what to write or how to answer the question - and there was often more than one subject set! Not only that, Rachel was smuggling books home that should never have left the school premises in order to finish her class work. Sometimes she worked solidly all weekend, even with our support and

Rachel struggled through that first year, after which we were grateful to learn that she was withdrawn from German lessons for her second year. After much discussion we eventually managed to persuade them to withdraw her from French as well and to substitute this with extra English lessons in their Remedial Unit.

True to her character, following her success with the recorder, Rachel now felt inspired to enrol herself for Clarinet lessons in the lunch hour, along with a couple of friends. We felt she was being overly ambitious but she seemed to enjoy the experience until her friends moved on to the next stage and she was left in the beginner's class. Fortunately, her music teacher had a dyslexic mother so proved extremely sympathetic and supportive towards Rachel, admiring her 'never say die' attitude, but eventually Rachel did give this up as a regrettable failure.

Following that, Rachel decided to try private singing lessons which finally proved to be her best musical venture. Apparently, she had a promising voice and had already gained some musical knowledge over the years. At last Rachel had found a musical outlet that could bring her satisfaction and she continued with this later in life by joining the local Musical Comedy Society where she succeeded and even enjoyed taking some leading roles. Although her Art work had suddenly improved out of all recognition Rachel would not consider this as an exam subject. History and Geography continued to prove hard for her as both involved so many new words; it was really like coping with another language for her but Maths and English still remained the hardest of all. Maths involved so many sequences of instructions that she could not follow, so she just plodded on in the lowest sets, which did nothing for her self-esteem. Even so, her teachers seemed to expect her to deal with concepts like negative and positive numbers and percentages that were way beyond her comprehension. Sometimes by modifying the teaching I could achieve some success at home but it took hours of working through practical examples to enable her to grasp a very basic concept. We didn't like seeing her having to work so hard but didn't know what else to do when she was so determined not to fail. Despite her teachers being convinced that she wasn't intelligent, Rachel was adamant that she would succeed in the end. Although Phil and I now felt out of our depth; with no one left to help us we could only continue to support her through the system, as best we could manage.

69

English, both oral and written, remained a headache for us all but Rachel refused for us to talk to her teacher about her problems. They rarely listened and never understood anyway! In times of crisis I resorted to writing a letter to the school unbeknown to Rachel or waiting until Open Evenings, which always proved the same; nothing but praise for her effort but *"Oh dear, she can't do it can she?"* Whenever we tried to explain the situation, and despite her IQ scoring of 120, which is defined as super-intelligent, we were constantly told that she wasn't as bright as we thought but not to worry as there were plenty more in the school just like her! Poor Rachel just didn't have the comprehension to cope with what was expected of her, which again made us think that she had a problem with language but where, how or from whom could we get the necessary help?

When Rachel began to enjoy reading for pleasure we were pleased to find some simplified versions of the children's classics that we bought for her, just as she was given a full copy of Macbeth to study for school! The whole situation was so absurd it seemed laughingly ridiculous; but we felt our hands were tied and obliged to go along with whatever they threw at us! Luckily, we managed to obtain a very simplified children's version of the basic story that she could use at home. We literally spent hours doing her homework and all the classwork that she was still smuggling out of school but it just resulted in more tears. In the end, at her request, we managed to find two sympathetic teachers who were willing to give her private tuition in Maths when required and English on a weekly basis.

Although Rachel's long-term memory had improved over the years, she still had difficulty in remembering dates and times or delivering a message correctly. She was 13 years old when she began to understand simple jokes but even then, she couldn't grasp the meaning of a punch line that involved a play on words or a homonym (a word sounding the same but having a different meaning e.g. 'bare' and 'bear.') One day we were all sitting down for breakfast when Gary asked us *"What did the baby chick say when the mother hen laid an orange?"* The answer was, *"Oh look what Mama laid,"* (to sound like marmalade.) Phil and I both laughed with him and thought it a good joke but Rachel became angry and stormed out of the room saying, *"I think that is a stupid joke. Everyone knows that hens lay eggs, not oranges!"* The whole punch line had been beyond her comprehension yet again. Instead of laughing then I felt more like crying as the whole situation seemed so sad.

Eventually, Rachel had to choose her topics to be studied to exam level. Maths and English were compulsory but she could choose up to six others. She chose Child Care, Needlework, Cookery and Nutrition which we felt would help her achieve her ambition in doing the highly esteemed National Nursery Education Board (NNEB) course in Child Care It was at this time that the new General Certificate of Secondary Education (GCSE) examinations were introduced and Rachel's year group were to be the 'guinea pigs.' Although I could see that this might be an advantage to Rachel as 60% of the marks in some exams were based on course work, thus relieving some of the pressure of a final exam, I was still worried that any allowances which an Educational Psychologist might arrange for the final papers, would not necessarily carry over into the new method of continual assessment.

Once more we felt at a loss as to how to help Rachel and there didn't seem to be any one to whom we could turn as Kevin had moved away and I had temporarily lost touch with my old friend Julie who was now living in another country. The careers person at school had more or less laughed in our faces when Rachel said that she wanted to do the well-respected NNEB course and said (I quote) *"You don't stand a hope in hell of getting into college; you'd be better off trying for a Youth Training Scheme run by the local council."* Rachel was clearly heart-broken by this rebuff but, as usual, responded with her phenomenal determination to succeed at all costs.

One day, when feeling particularly low, I pulled out my old diaries, in which I had written down all my thoughts and any significant events about Rachel, in an attempt to try and comprehend her problems. So far, I had only written things in them as they'd occurred, along with my monthly reviews and plans but had never sat down to actually read them from beginning to end. As I now read my entries it became apparent how often I had written that Rachel just didn't seem to understand things. I had even queried a language problem with Kevin Brown at our very first meeting but as with everyone else, he had brushed it aside as being unlikely. At one time I had even queried if Rachel might be dyslexic and joined the local support group to try and identify with their problems but found that although dyslexics had similar difficulties with sequencing letters or ideas, they could usually understand conversations and explain their thoughts orally; their main problem was with the written word.

I then resolved to do my best to acquire a full language assessment for Rachel but knew that this was easier said than done and, as expected, we met with nothing but obstacles along the way. We battled with Educational Psychologists and Speech and Language Therapists for nearly 2 years, both locally and in London but they were all unable to assess her because Rachel was over 11 years old but not yet an adult. Although, on the evidence of a few tests that were done locally they said that she was predisposed to having a language problem but nothing more conclusive was achieved.

It was quite by coincidence that I befriended a new dinner lady called Brenda at work who had a daughter with a Severe Language Disorder that wished to join Brownies. I explained how I had coped with similar problems with Rachel who was now a Young Leader at a local Brownie Pack and would be only too pleased to help her daughter. In conversation I happened to mention the diaries I had kept on Rachel that Brenda asked to read. Whilst she had them Brenda took it upon herself to show them to her daughter's Headteacher at the Unit for Children with Language Impairment. On returning the diaries Brenda told me what she had done and that the teacher was convinced that Rachel presented as a classic case of a child with language impairment!

I didn't know what to think at that stage but agreed to go with Brenda to the next Afasic (Association for all Speech Impaired Children) meeting: a support group for parents of children with speech and language problems. I was told that there would be a talk that evening by a Psychologist on how to recognise language impairment in 4 year olds and that I would have a chance to meet the teacher who had read my diaries. It was a shame that Phil couldn't come along as well but he said he was happy to stay at home with the children and thought I was better placed to understand the talk anyway.

That evening I sat and listened like someone stunned as the Psychologist proceeded to describe our daughter, exactly as she had been at that age! I felt both relieved and excited to know that at last I really knew what her problem was, without any doubt or uncertainty; but how to get them properly acknowledged or the necessary help for her was another matter! However, it seemed that answer was also on hand as Brenda's friend, (the Headteacher of a Unit for Children with Language Impairment), was willing to refer Rachel to her friend who was the Chief Speech and Language Therapist at Guy's Hospital in London, for a full language assessment. I could not believe my luck. Maybe our struggle was nearly over at last.

At the end of Rachel's fourth year in Senior School we reviewed all her exam subjects with her teachers. Her best subject was Child Care but even in that she had problems with the medical terminology and basic biology related to problems in pregnancy and contraception. Cookery was OK but the theory for Nutrition involved yet another language for her that needed a great deal of work on food values. For this, I ended up making her a simple picture book depicting all the different food categories and their functions. Needlework was fine and Typing was adequate but slow, for which we bought her a typewriter so that she could practice at home to keep up with her peers. Maths and English were in hand with the extra tuition but we really weren't happy with the pressure she felt when working at History and World Studies.

The school had insisted that these were added to Rachel's syllabus to broaden what they described as a limited range of topics. Obviously, these subjects were way beyond her comprehension, even though we knew it was a reasonable curriculum for an average 16 year old. Personally, I found it easier to discuss the General Election or the Chernobyl disaster with the deaf junior children at work than I did such issues with Rachel. Even though she was living through these events, it was like talking about an alien subject with her. They might as well have occurred on another planet. It all seemed so futile and unnecessary for her to study these things at this stage in her life. We were just as frustrated as Rachel.

Every evening and whole weekends were spent on her homework to ensure that she kept up to date with all the assignments and projects required for her courses, which we felt was too heavy a workload for her. Eventually, as her World Studies and History teachers admitted that she was likely to fail in both those exams they agreed to our request that she could drop these subjects, giving her more time to concentrate on those in which she hoped to succeed. It was also agreed that she could have some work experience at a local nursery for children with disabilities, which not only gave her some relief from studying, but also gave her some practical support for her child care projects.

At 15 years old Rachel was still naive and immature but was beginning to show some independence away from the family unit. Although her language was still a problem, she had developed a few coping strategies of her own, so would now dismiss a conversation if she became muddled or tongue-tied, instead of reverting to the old tantrums. However, it could take her up to 10 minutes for her to recall a word that she needed like 'soup.' At other times she would say, *"We are going to do a ballet dance in the next show."* Now she'd been doing ballet dancing and shows since she was three years old but, on that occasion, she'd meant that they'd be doing a classical ballet dance and wearing tutus although she couldn't find the words to say that. She also often muddled things like similar road names such as East Street and East Ham Road which could cause problems when going about the town independently. In general, Rachel's language was basic but adequate as she tended to speak in simple sentences but she always had problems when she wanted to explain something specific.

Her understanding was also adequate for everyday life but she was out of her depth in school unless she could relate the subject to her own life experiences or the subject was supported either visually or practically. Likewise, with her written work, Rachel always seemed to answer questions with a simple sentence even when half a page or at least a paragraph was required. I remember one incident in Cookery when she was asked to write a short essay on why she had chosen to cook a certain menu, for which she had already gained the top mark of A in the practical session. Rachel submitted her answer in just one simple sentence: *"I chose these foods because they were good for you."* Hardly sufficient for a GCSE pass!

Even after she had worked on a class lesson, repeated it with her private tutor and spent more time at home with our support, she could still only hand in an essay on one piece of A4 paper, full of grammatical errors, full stops and capital letters scattered haphazardly over the page, spelling errors and sometimes even incomprehensible gibberish! For example, Rachel submitted the following essay, after just such support and guidance, written in her immature handwriting, as a GCSE piece. It has been copied here exactly as submitted showing her grammar, sentence structure, use of capital letters and punctuation:

Essay on Schools.   *16.10.87*

The schools were very different 100 years ago to what they are now.

Lessons were conducted in a different way they had object Lessons which were   asking   Questions about a certain object.   The children when asked a question all answered together.   This is parrot fashion.   Parrot fashion is when everybody answers the same question together for instance The teacher may ask.   What is the capital of france the children altogether will answer paris.

If the child was asked this question on his / her own they might not be able to answer or if the child was asked what is 2 x 4 they would probably not be able to answer without going through the table.

If also the children never learnt as much because they only had one person teaching a whole group of them most of the time and although they had the older children teaching younger ones sometimes.

Children learnt a few Lessons like History, Geography, English and Arithmatic and then only what the teachers knew, which was only a limited amount, or what was in the book. that the teachers were given.   If the children gave a wrong answer to what the teachers had in the book then the teachers were completely thrown for what to say next.

At the school the condisions of the children were poor they were dirty and about two out of fifteen were well dressed with faces washed etc their were also not very clean school the children were all squashed together with about 60 to one class and the teachers had quite a lot of children of all ages together the boys on one side and the girls on another.

The schools were quite strict as well They had to read from the Bible and Learn it.   The schools also had a cane. and if anyone did anything wrong they used it to be hit by the cane.

Chapter Ten

Diagnosis and Recognition

In the February before Rachel took her GCSEs, we were offered an appointment at Guy's Hospital in The Newcomen Centre that we gladly accepted. We arrived on time and were seen by a Paediatrician, Clinical Psychologist and a Speech and Language Therapist who all asked Rachel questions about her work at school and what she found difficult in subjects like Needlework, to which she replied, *"I find the patterns difficult."* When one of them said that he thought everyone found those a little difficult to sort out at times, I really felt as though we were being patronised yet again! After about 20 minutes of general chat we were told that they didn't think Rachel had any major problems and we could go. We both went outside feeling very angry and frustrated, especially Rachel who cried because she felt that they hadn't believed in her. We had hoped for so much more from that appointment but left with nothing yet again.

We were therefore astonished a few weeks later, to receive a letter from Pamela Page, the Chief Speech and Language Therapist at Guy's Hospital who said she would be interested in seeing Rachel herself and offered us yet another appointment at the centre at the end of May. Obviously, we agreed but both Phil and I were puzzled by this strange turn of events. We could only think that although the two Doctors weren't interested in Rachel, the Therapist must have seen something that might be worth investigating.

We set off in good time from the south coast to London, expecting to arrive with half an hour to spare, giving us plenty of time to literally cross the road from the railway station to the hospital. However, there was a problem on the line and the train came to a grinding halt for nearly an hour just outside the station, making us unavoidably late for the appointment! How could fate be so cruel? After waiting all these years for this assessment, I was desperate that nothing should go wrong now. We therefore ran across the road, arriving breathless at the centre nearly half an hour late. Fortunately, the staff there understood that this was not our fault so, as Pamela was already available and waiting for us, we were shown straight into her room at approximately three o'clock. When Pamela had finished taking a detailed history of Rachel's general and language development, she chatted to Rachel in a relaxed fashion to assess her conversational abilities and explained the special tests that she wanted to use. Rachel seemed quite relaxed, happy and cooperative although the tests seemed endless. She was shown lots of pictures of everyday objects but couldn't always recall their names so said things like 'skirt' for 'kilt' even though she had a kilt herself and knew the name. At other times she would say *"I can't remember,"* describe what she'd do with it or when shown something like a bracelet she indicated with her hands how she would put it on her wrist.

In the next test Rachel was shown sets of four pictures and asked to indicate which one Pamela was describing. At first these were easy like *"Show me the cat on the chair"* but gradually these became harder. When Pamela said *"Show me the cow being chased by the boy"* Rachel pointed to the cow actually chasing the boy instead. She was then asked to repeat simple sentences that gradually became more complex and asked to give a rhyming word to words that Pamela was saying. Rachel was told a story about a dog in eleven short sentences and was asked to retell it but could only remember half and so it went on. Numerous other tests followed involving her listening skills and ability with rhythm. All the way through testing Pamela was asking Rachel how she felt and how she had coped with each test to discover what strategies, if any, Rachel had used.

Eventually Pamela finished her comprehensive examination and explained how Rachel had done in all the various tests. She said that although it was obvious that Rachel had a Semantic Pragmatic Language Disorder that was on the beginning of the Autistic Spectrum, she had to some extent, learnt to live with this by using her own little coping strategies. Pamela went on to say that Rachel's ability at 16 years of age was comparable with that of a 12 - 14 year old and that her problems were in both understanding language and using it herself. Her main problems were in mentally sorting out what was being said to her involving grammar, sequencing words, understanding their meaning and recalling them to use herself. When I asked about the cause of this Pamela explained that this was still unknown at that time.

Pamela then gave us some advice on how to improve Rachel's coping strategies and as we were planning to move to Cornwall in July, after Rachel left school, she said she would write to the Head of the Speech and Language Therapy department in Plymouth to arrange therapy sessions with our new Health Authority. Pamela also recommended that we considered getting Rachel statemented by the Education Authority to ensure that she had all the necessary help she needed if she wanted to go to College. Pamela remarked about the immense amount of effort that Rachel had shown in order to do the tests to the best of her ability and said that she should definitely have been assessed and probably have attended a special school for children with language impairment when she was 4 years old! As we were preparing to leave, Pamela told us that she was surprised at how well Rachel had managed over the years. When we actually left her room, it was nearly 6pm! Everywhere was in darkness and Pamela had to unlock the main doors to let us out. What a difference from all our other experiences; nobody had ever gone to so much trouble for us before.

I had a multitude of mixed emotions but mainly felt both humble and grateful to Pamela for all her time, compassion and professional skills. I was also extremely confused, frustrated and angry about the situation we were now in. It was just three days since Rachel had taken her last GCSE exam yet it had taken until now for us to obtain the diagnosis we'd been searching for since she'd been born! Consequently, Rachel had struggled needlessly through the mainstream educational system having all her problems disregarded for most of the time while we had been either patronised or rudely ignored by all those professionals over the years. I think we both left Guy's Hospital stunned by our wide range of emotions.

Rachel was extremely drained and exhausted after the extensive testing but was relieved to have a diagnosis at last as it instantly gave her a feeling of self-worth and hope for the future. On the train home she began to quietly cry with relief, saying that at least she now knew that she wasn't 'stupid' as nothing had upset her more than being thought 'thick' by her peers and especially her teachers. Rachel had often come home and cried because of her problems at school, someone hadn't understood her or she had known that her teachers hadn't believed us when we'd tried to explain a situation on her behalf. At last she could now hold her head high with self-respect. Personally, although I was relieved and grateful to have a diagnosis at last,

I was actually shocked to hear that Rachel's disorder was on the Autistic Spectrum. I think, to be honest, that my initial reaction to this was denial until I remembered how Rachel hadn't been able to understand jokes, couldn't cope with change and all her unaccountable fears and phobias. As I thought about this on the train home, it all gradually began to make sense. Simultaneously though, I also felt somewhat vindictive towards the professionals that had dealt with us in the past. When we arrived home and told Phil the result of our visit, he was equally frustrated and angry about all the unnecessary suffering and struggling that Rachel had endured over the previous years. It also seemed unbelievable that the special school Pamela had said would have been best for Rachel was only 12 miles from our home; instead we had been continually either patronised or disbelieved by most of her mainstream teachers.

It took me a long time to come to terms with the needless hurt and humiliation that Rachel had suffered because we had asked Kevin Brown to do her original assessment when she was 6 years old instead of our friend Julie who was a competent Speech and Language Therapist. To say that I felt guilty seemed inadequate to describe my feelings, knowing that we'd obviously made the wrong decision all those years ago and could have made Rachel's life so much easier if only we'd let Julie carry out those tests. I consoled myself by rationalising that Rachel was probably a stronger person as a result of her experiences but that really didn't lessen my guilt. She was certainly very sensitive to other people's feelings and needs, which could well have been due to all her own struggles and emotional difficulties over the years. Thankfully though, we had all been given the strength and ability to deal with everything. The biggest problem now was to get this diagnosis accepted by the education system and try to gain entry into college.

Knowing that we would be moving to Liskeard, in Cornwall, as soon as she finished school, Rachel applied for the NNEB courses in both Plymouth and Saltash (Cornwall) Colleges. However, thanks to a letter sent from her Senior School, written by her Head of House, Saltash initially didn't offer her an interview. I think I will always remember the day that letter arrived. Rachel picked it up and opened it excitedly after seeing the postmark, expecting to see a date for an interview but instead she was devastated on reading the letter enclosed. It simply said that in view of the letter sent from her school it didn't really seem worthwhile interviewing her!

Rachel was heartbroken - but I was angry to think that someone could be judged in such a way and not even be given the chance to prove themselves worthy of consideration. Especially when we discovered that the letter had been written by Rachel's old Head of House who had never even met her, let alone taught her!

Phil and I therefore decided to do our best to make them reconsider their decision so rallied around to send off references from her private tutors, employers, Guiders, including her Guide Commissioner who had always admired Rachel's fortitude and various other people who had seen her working with children. We also sent an explanatory letter and a request to review her application, which thankfully they did. Meanwhile Plymouth automatically agreed to interview her as they had various levels of child care courses available for students. Nevertheless, Rachel was adamant that she would only ever consider the NNEB course. Sadly, but not unexpectedly, she failed both entrance exams but was able to accept this outcome as she knew this was due to her own inability rather than a letter of condemnation from someone who really didn't know her. Although no doubt that letter to the College could well have influenced their judgement. Rachel therefore applied for a place in the 6th form at Liskeard School for

one year, in her new local town, and planned to reapply for the NNEB course the following year.

During this difficult period a cherished event occurred when Rachel was chosen by a close friend to be her bridesmaid.

I spent many hours on the telephone trying to initiate Rachel's statementing process but West Sussex didn't want to know as she was 16 years old even though statementing was valid until a student was 19 years of age. Obviously, Cornwall couldn't initiate things until Rachel had entered one of their schools and unfortunately, I didn't know then that I could have initiated this process myself as a parent! One thing I did manage to do though, whilst still in West Sussex was have an interview with the Careers Adviser for the Handicapped (his title at that time) in order to gain some information regarding Rachel's rights should she fail to achieve her aim once we were in Cornwall. I also 'phoned the Head of the only senior school in the country for pupils with language impairment, to ask for advice on how to get Rachel into college. I was told that she should be exempt from the entrance exams and that statementing was essential to ensure that any appropriate help Rachel needed was provided. This was also confirmed by The Afasic Association in London but I was unable to obtain any satisfactory responses from County Hall.

That summer we moved to Cornwall and Rachel received her GCSE results in the August, which were surprisingly good and reflected the enormous hard work that she had done. Her worst result of an F grade, was understandably in Maths, with an E in Home Economics that was probably due to the problems she'd had in understanding the theory and nutritional values. We were pleased to learn that she'd passed her Typing exams and obtained a D in Needlework but were amazed to find that she'd gained a D for English, which was probably thanks to all her private tuition. Best of all was the fact that she'd gained a C in Child Care!

A week before school was due to start, we were invited to look around the 6th Form area at Liskeard School and meet the Head of the department. He was a kind and caring man, who showed an interest in Rachel's problems and asked for a copy of the report from Guy's Hospital. This different attitude in Cornwall compared to West Sussex was something we were soon to get used to and for which we were immensely grateful. In fact, I began to lose count of the number of copies of that report that were sent off in various directions to so many different people's files. It was wonderfully reassuring to see how everything was just slotting into place now.

Rachel began her Speech and Language Therapy sessions in a building near the school at 9am once a week and I went with her for the first session for moral support. As I thought she was now able to cope with these sessions by herself I suggested she went alone for the next one but was disappointed to find that she had forgotten to attend and gone straight into school as usual instead. We therefore encouraged her to make her own apologies and confirm her next appointment, which she did, but subsequently forgot that appointment as well even though we'd reminded her of where to go as she left home. This was so typical of her that we decided to let the people trying to help her, see how she performed normally.

81

We felt there was no point in masking her problems by helping her avoid them in this situation. We therefore insisted that she should again make her own arrangements but as she took so many days to pluck up the courage to make the 'phone call, I meanwhile, secretly 'phoned the therapist to explain what had happened. Meanwhile, we were sent an appointment for a school medical, which we assumed was routine for all new entrants. Instead, it transpired that it was due to the excellent communication between all the various departments down here, as we discovered when the Doctor said that she'd heard that Rachel had missed two therapy sessions. She asked what the problem had been and on learning about Rachel's difficulties, she suggested that the appointments be changed to 9.15am. In this way, Rachel could avoid following the throng into school and be more likely to follow her intended route. Thankfully this worked well with Rachel successfully attending the planned sessions and thus started learning new strategies to compensate for her problems.

We were impressed during this first half term to not only meet all Rachel's new teachers, who all wanted to 'bend over backwards' to help her, but also many others involved with her education. Phil and I were therefore invited to a meeting with the Head of the Remedial Department and the Educational Psychologist to discuss Rachel's report from Guy's Hospital and how they envisaged helping her to succeed over the next year, by ensuring that she gained a place on the NNEB course at the local college. Both these ladies had an amazing amount of empathy and understanding. They also showed wonderful commitment to their work and we couldn't have wished for better support. For the first time in Rachel's life we felt we could trust the professionals enough to leave it all up to them to deal with and confident that they wouldn't let us down.

Appointments were made for both of them to meet Rachel individually in the following week, after which all the cogs seemed to spring into action and continued to turn satisfactorily. As the help available was so personally geared to meet Rachel's needs, we didn't feel the need to pursue the statementing issue now that we were in Cornwall. Although we still watched closely, prepared to jump into action should the need arise it thankfully never did. There was even another offer of help that endeared us to all these caring professionals, which was when Rachel's new English teacher came to our house to ask how he could best help Rachel improve her

English grade in case she needed a Grade C to enter college. He volunteered to give her extra coaching in the lunch hour and made her promise to see him at any break time if she was ever unsure of any class work. There were other recommendations and offers of further coaching plus special concessions, but Rachel now had all the help she needed and preferred to build up a normal relationship with her new peers, so although these offers were gratefully declined, they were very much appreciated.

During that year Rachel not only passed her driving test but improved in confidence generally, academically and socially, so much so, that she actually won a place at the local college for the next NNEB course on her own merit. It was agreed that she would be exempt from the entrance exam; in as much as she would not be judged on the marks, although they asked her to sit it along with the other applicants to give them an idea of her ability. She passed with 64%!

That year Rachel not only passed her driving test but successfully gained passes in all her school subjects, managing to go up a grade in Maths to E, gained a D in Business studies and surprised us by gaining a D in Geography; a subject with its own specific language that she could not have coped with previously. Her best pass was a C in Social Studies, which again amazed us all, considering that this had also been dropped from her previous GCSE syllabus. She passed Stage 1 in Office Practice and gained the Certificate of Pre-Vocational Education but sadly maintained a D in English despite her teacher's best efforts. Everything looked set for the future now and we were very proud of her.

Chapter Eleven

The Chance of a Future

Rachel entered College in September 1989 with about eighteen other girls aged between 16 and 25 years of age. She immediately gelled with a group of three other girls, developing a special friendship with one that remained until the girl herself sadly died a few years ago. Although she was never actually statemented, Rachel's two main tutors in College requested a copy of the report from Guy's Hospital and asked their Educational Psychologist to do a further assessment and report. Interestingly, this was the same lady that had first seen Rachel on her arrival at Liskeard 6th Form and her three page report proved to be invaluable.

It stated that Rachel was of good intelligence but was slow at processing her thoughts; not by lack of intellectual ability but due to sequencing problems. It also said that Rachel had a good vocabulary but suffered from word finding problems, good intelligence but was slow at processing her thoughts; not by lack of intellectual but suffered from word finding problems. Her test results were very varied as she was able to use some well-developed strategies in certain tests, whereas in others, although she had given the right answer, she had exceeded the time limit thus making the score invalid. Rachel was noted to have obvious difficulty when needing to reorganise information in her memory, as required when doing multiple-choice type questions. She displayed no reading problems but her spelling was weak for her age due to the sequencing problems although her errors were only minor, making it easy for the reader to know what was intended.

The report concluded that Rachel had all the necessary skills in reading, writing and spelling for the course and that the examining process should be well within her capabilities. The Psychologist stated that she had difficulty in commenting on Rachel's internal thought processes needed to retrieve information from her memory, organise, plan and write an answer in response to a question. The report explained that this process would take Rachel a long time and she would also be hampered by tiredness or stress. The Psychologist acknowledged that she was even aware of Rachel taking a long time to consider her response before answering a question in general conversation. On reflection, after reading that report I was reminded of the comments made by one of Rachel's Junior School teachers after watching her struggling to do a multiple-choice paper and had remarked upon her slow thought processes. Unfortunately, her problems were not being acknowledged then but he must have been a very perceptive man.

The College sent both these reports to the NNEB examining panel asking for extra time and any other suitable allowances to be made for such things as poor spelling. Consequently, Rachel would only be judged on the content of her answers provided that the examiners could clearly understand what she meant. The College also suggested that Rachel sat some mock exams at the end of her first year along with the finalists to familiarise her with the setting. Though her marks were not recorded, her tutors used the information gained to help improve Rachel's skills during her final year, ready for sitting her own final exams. Again, we felt we couldn't have asked for more so were happy to leave the situation in the hands of these obviously caring and experienced people.

Rachel loved College and coped remarkably well, especially with all the practical work on all her various placements, although she did suffer from extreme anxiety at times when travelling alone on a new route even though we had always rehearsed it with her to make things less stressful, or when she was unsure of what would be expected of her in a new placement or setting. Nonetheless, her natural determination and courage usually saw her through such situations. Her main problems now lay in keeping up with all the projects and assignments and Rachel's tutors were aware that she still needed some support from us. Still, they said that was acceptable as all the students gained their information from various resources and they would be able to monitor her ability by the essays she produced in College. She was also allowed to use a word processor at home which proved a great asset as she didn't have to rewrite all her work several times before handing it in.

Nevertheless, there were still times when I would sit up in bed late at night to read through a book for her, highlighting or making notes on all the relevant pages and paragraphs to help her make a quicker start on an essay. At other times when she was tired, she would lie in bed and dictate the facts that she wanted recorded. I would then write it up with all the correct grammar and spelling so that she could copy it out the next day. Even with the word processor Rachel still needed help in organising a presentation or extending her, all too brief answers on an assignment or placement that she had done.

Phil also became involved at times when we worked our way through brochures, leaflets and magazines, cutting out pictures to illustrate her work to ensure that she met a deadline. Rachel did not want to make use of her concession of extra time if she could avoid it as she always wanted to be treated the same as her peers, which we respected. Only once did she need to ask for extra time, when a project was handed in two days late. At the end of the exhausting but enjoyable two years Rachel sat the examination alongside her peers, after which it seemed strange not to have the constant pressure of another assignment hanging over all our heads. We now had nothing to do but await the results with bated breath.

Despite all her problems it seems ironic that Rachel was the first one on her course to secure a full-time post. She had been working for a family in the

holidays with a little boy called Toby, who was severely disabled by Cerebral Palsy, Epilepsy and Asthma, but the family now felt that they required a full-time live-in nanny. Rachel was their first choice as she already knew the child and she was pleased to accept. This appointment especially appealed to Rachel as she would be involved with learning the Hungarian Conductive Education method for treating Cerebral Palsy; first used at the Peto Institute, but now being used in Britain. We were also relieved that not only would she be spared the trauma of interviews until she was more confident and mature but we thought it would relieve some of the pressure hanging over her during the examination period. Not long after leaving College Rachel settled into her new regime extremely well and everyone that knew her was amazed at the newly found confidence that she began to display.

Early in August the long-awaited envelope landed on the mat beneath our letter box containing her examination results. As it had arrived a few days earlier than expected I didn't know what to expect so simply placed it on the released and asked if an envelope had arrived and would we open it for her? Suddenly the moment of truth had come and I felt very confused. All the feelings of frustration, apprehension and concern that we had experienced over the years seemed to be suspended in the air. I had always felt confident that she would cope with this course but now I began to wonder if we had really done the right thing by supporting her desire to aim so high. Would we now have to tell her that she had failed? I desperately hoped not! Surely life couldn't be so cruel? She had worked so hard and come so far, surely only success could come now. I'd had complete faith in her up until that moment but suddenly I full of doubt and felt guilty in case Rachel should now receive yet another 'knock' in life.

As all those thoughts flashed through my mind, I found I couldn't bring myself to open that envelope so gave it to Phil and waited while he did the ominous deed. Time seemed to stand still for the few seconds it took him to do this, look at the card and read out the result. *She had passed!* I cannot explain the feelings of relief and joy that swept over me at that moment. It seemed hard to believe that all those years of struggling and fighting for Rachel were actually over. Had we really reached our goal at last? It seemed like a dream but there we all were, awake and talking to each other on the telephone. After telling Rachel the good news we said we would take the card straight round to her so that she could see it for herself. Then Phil and I just stood and hugged each other for some minutes, after which I began to cry. It was as if all the pent-up emotions of the last few years were flowing out of me. Rachel had realised her dream at last. She had always wanted to do the NNEB course, which she had successfully completed - but now she had passed their exam as well! We were so proud of her. I was as ecstatic as though my child had passed out of Oxford or Cambridge with a first-class honours degree! To us it was just as great an achievement and I wanted to tell the world about it!

When we arrived at Rachel's new home, we all hugged each other and cried again. Even her new boss joined in and offered us a glass of wine to cele-brate the event. She then told Rachel that she could have the evening off to accompany us to a party to celebrate properly. Following Rachel's success at College we were even prouder to learn that they had now decided to take on other students with similar problems; the first one being a student with dyslexia on the very next course; a fitting end to all our struggles and was good to know that our battle had not only proved worthwhile for Rachel but had also opened the door for others.

Chapter Twelve

What Happened Next?

Rachel enjoyed working with this family for several years, including accompanying Toby as his classroom assistant, four days a week at a mainstream nursery and on the remaining day at a special school run by SCOPE, (a national charity that campaigns for equality for people with disabilities). When Toby entered full time school Rachel decided to change jobs but this time chose to work as a Nanny for a baby girl with normal development, whose parents were both in full time employment. Again, she stayed until the child started school when she helped to set up and run a nursery attached to a local school. Other jobs included working as an Assistant at a Montessori Nursery and as a Classroom Assistant for the Local Education Authority at a Primary School for Children with Moderate Learning Disabilities before settling as a Nursery Nurse in the community with the local Health Visitors where she worked happily for 16 years.

More recently, now that her own children have grown up, Rachel is working for the local council as a Family Support Worker. Although Rachel began work as a live-in Nanny, she returned home briefly before living independently in the local town with another girl of similar age. We were thrilled at this display of independence and hoped things would go well for them but sadly the other girl had to leave and Rachel returned home once more.

Throughout her life Rachel continued to enjoy dancing and local amateur musical theatre, in which she first performed aged 3 years. Following our move to Cornwall in 1988 she immediately joined the local amateur Musical Comedy or Operatic Societies, depending on where she was living, as a member of their cast and performing as a dancer, part of the chorus or even taking leading roles.

She is currently working with one of the leading Amateur Operatic Societies in Cornwall for whom she became their Choreographer, before moving on to become Assistant Producer, a role in which she continues to this day. It seems as though Rachel has not looked back since leaving education and has progressed at her own pace both socially and professionally in areas where she's felt confident and comfortable, which has been wonderful to witness. In fact, following the success of the first two editions of this book she has even made a speech, to about 3,000 delegates, at one of the Afasic Conferences.

When Rachel initially told us that she had a boyfriend we were thrilled for her but as it became clear that he was a rather dominating man with a strong character, we did have concerns that sadly only grew with time. Nevertheless, Rachel seemed to be oblivious of this and once again realised her own dream by having a beautiful wedding in 1997 and even went on to have two precious daughters. Sadly though, our original concerns were confirmed as we knew she wasn't really happy in this marriage. Having worked so hard, for so long, to help Rachel become independent, it was now heart-breaking to watch her gradually becoming more and more submissive to this man, although she herself bravely tried to hide this from us for some years. Eventually, Rachel confessed to realising that despite how well she was succeeding both socially and at work; it was only at home where she was failing and things felt wrong. She then admitted that she had thought of leaving her husband three times in the past but had now decided she could no longer continue in the marriage due to emotional, psychological and financial abuse. Although we obviously agreed to support her decision, as we had with the marriage despite our concerns, we knew it was unwise as her parents, for us to give her any advice. We therefore put her in touch with the 24 hour helpline at Women's Aid and Women's Refuge, whose advice she gratefully followed with our support. Consequently, Rachel came to our house one day as planned with both girls and subsequently became divorced in 2012.

With all her usual determination, Rachel only stayed with us for a few months until she found rental accommodation within the girl's school catchment area to prevent any unnecessary changes or disruption for them. She then began looking for a suitable house to buy and was lucky enough to find a lovely three- bedroomed house with a good garden in the right area for the girls' schools. I'm afraid the next few years were dominated by a custody battle that Rachel thankfully won, as their father wanted the girls to live with him 100%; even stating that Rachel had a learning disability and was incapable of parenting them! This was despite the fact that Rachel was actually teaching parent craft and behaviour management to parents at work as a Health Visitor assistant. However, the girls claimed that they wanted to live with their mother and just visit their father, which was eventually achieved after several court hearings. Thankfully this still continues today as both girls live happily with their mother, while seeing their father about once a week, although the eldest girl, Bethany is now due to leave home for Kingston University to study Psychology. Meanwhile the younger daughter, Katie is still living at home with Rachel and attending her local College one day a week as part of her hairdressing apprenticeship.

It is interesting to note that while the girls were both young, I watched them like a hawk for any signs indicating that they may have inherited Rachel's language disorder - but saw none. There were some behavioural problems, especially with Bethany like head-banging at 5 years of age, and self-harming at about 11 years old. Notably both girls also wet the bed until 5 years old, but we thought all this was probably due to the abusive atmosphere of their family home.

Bethany also displayed some anti-social behaviour like slapping another toddler if they didn't do as she wished, was rather a fussy child and had a particularly limited diet but otherwise showed no specific problems at that stage, apart from hand flapping when she was excited, which we dismissed as an endearing trait. However, as she entered adolescence Bethany began to have lots of time off school for various health issues including asthmatic episodes, even resulting in overnight hospitalisation despite being well oxygenated and non-pathological headaches, for which she took strong medication although the Paediatrician could find no known cause. She also developed high sensitivity to light, sound, smell, taste and touch, that became exacerbated when she was tired or unwell, making life particularly stressful at times, which in turn could lead to panic attacks and even 'melt downs' at times.

One day when Rachel was watching a TV programme about girls with

Autism, she wondered if Bethany might actually be Autistic, when Rachel heard someone in the programme seemingly describing her own daughter! Rachel just sat there with tears running down her face and feeling guilty that she had failed Bethany in some way by not realising this before. Nevertheless, it took a further two years before an assessment was obtained and five more months before Bethany was finally diagnosed with High Functioning Autism, often referred to as Asperger's Syndrome.

By now Bethany was already attending College where the staff were very supportive and helpful, although her first year did seem to be more about coping with the transition from school and perhaps coming to terms with her diagnosis. Consequently, by staying an extra year at College Bethany is now flourishing, having passed all her necessary A level exams plus her driving test, works part time at a local supermarket and can't wait to start her University course this summer. Interestingly, Bethany has always enjoyed dancing like her mother and is also a member of the same amateur Operatic Society where she is one of their leading dancers.

Regrettably Bethany's father had difficulty in establishing a good relationship with her, resulting in awkward visits at times and Bethany needing her sister present for moral support when meeting with him. He also found it hard to accept Bethany's Autism, preferring to state that her problems were all simply due to the way that Rachel handled her or even just in Rachel's imagination.

Meanwhile, towards the end of Junior School, Katie was diagnosed as having a Semantic Language Disorder with a weak auditory memory (a minor version of Rachel's own problems), as she has difficulty following verbal instructions. Although little was done to help her there, the staff at Senior School proved much more effective and supportive, resulting in Katie gaining good passes in all her GCSE exams and flourishing since entering College. Although Katie often became frustrated when she didn't comprehend something, she did not seem to have any social problems. Instead she went through school befriending any of her peer group in need; even taking them home if she felt it necessary. In fact, Rachel received a 'phone call one day from Social Services asking if she could keep one of Katie's friends for a week as it wasn't considered safe for her to go home! Furthermore, far from having a pragmatic problem Katie loves writing film scripts in her spare time and dreams of having them produced one day.

Sadly, since losing the court cases for the girls to live with him, their father has not been involved with either of their upbringings. Consequently, Rachel has had to work hard to cope as the single mother of two daughters, who not only have their own special needs but were also angry and hurt by their father's behaviour at times, resulting in them both needing counselling and Katie even being referred to the Child and Adolescent Mental Health Service.

Meanwhile Rachel has simultaneously managed to hold responsible positions at work while maintaining the family home. Obviously, this has not been easy for her and she is often tired but somehow, with all her usual fortitude and determination she has succeeded against all odds to triumph as usual in the end.

Above: Rachel with daughters Bethany and baby Katie

Left: Top to bottom - Me, Bethany, Rachel and Katie on a log flume

Katie, Bethany and Rachel at Kingston University

Rachel with her brother Gary and Parents

Appendix I

Hints for parents

In order to cope with Rachel's screaming, and frustration tantrums I found it best to 'switch off' emotionally. This was not always easy to do especially in the early days but eventually I was able to think, 'Here we go again,' and go through the motions of holding and rocking her until she calmed enough to be reasoned with. I repeat: this was much easier said than done but it is better to stay in control of the situation than it is to 'join in!' When a child is so upset because it is frightened, confused or frustrated it needs someone to give them security and make them feel safe. The last thing it needs is for the adult to 'crack up' as well.

As Rachel had to be taught everything through touch or experience (tactile or kinaesthetic teaching,) we used practical apparatus as much as possible, hence Phil made the counting rods to teach her tens and units and the toy library was an invaluable resource. Telling and showing just didn't work for Rachel. I therefore refer to the old Chinese proverb:

> *Tell me and I forget,*
>
> *Show me and I see,*
>
> *Involve me and I remember.*

The left and right patterning movement in crawling is believed to be an important preliminary exercise for reading and writing.

Before learning literacy, children need lots of physical experiences such as crawling, hopping, skipping and climbing, in order to become well coordinated. This is because the large motor movements need to be established before learning to control the fine motor movements needed for threading, cutting, tracing, drawing, colouring and ultimately writing.

Rachel also had to learn to manage her hand-eye co-ordination. We began by using a large beach ball at close range and slowly moving further away. Then gradually introduced smaller balls until she could cope with a bat and ball.

A child needs to understand its own body image and where it is in space to fully understand where one thing is in relation to another; also important in literacy. We began by getting her to lie down on a large piece of paper on the floor and drew all around her body. We then encouraged her to do this to us. We then made plasticine models, always making sure that the neck was included and eventually progressed to learning how to draw people.

Understanding prepositions (place words like on, in, under, etc.) is important before learning about the position of letters on a line e.g. on, under or above plus the relationship of each letter to another for reading and spelling. To teach this we played games with large cardboard boxes in the garden and on playground equipment, talking all the time about going in a tunnel, up the steps, down a slide or under a seat, etc.

We taught Rachel to write correctly by using her index (pointing) finger to trace the shapes on our backs, in sand and any other rough surface. In this way the message reached the brain through the sense of touch and movement, after which the pencil became an extension of the finger.

Many children with learning difficulties have failed to develop a dominant side, like Rachel. As we believed she was mainly right handed we decided to make her consciously aware of always using her right hand for pointing (including using the correct pointing finger), picking things up, etc.

To make Rachel right footed we taught her to play hop-scotch, always hopping on the right foot and even encouraged her to play this when walking down the pavement by using the paving slab patterns (without the stone of course!) Other children may prefer playing football using their appropriate foot depending on their dominant side.

To make her right eyed we encouraged Rachel to play with a kaleidoscope, telescope or any other type of peephole activity for about 5 minutes twice a day.

Dancing helped Rachel with both coordination and sequencing whilst also becoming more aware of her lefts and rights. The repeated practicing of movement sequences also proved a bonus in helping to train her memory whilst performing on stage worked wonders for her self-esteem and confidence.

Appendix II

Helpful Information

• The opening sentence of the 1989 Children's Act stated that 'The welfare of the child is paramount' and that parents have responsibilities towards their children to see that everything necessary for their child's welfare is carried out.

• The 2004 Children Act reinforced this by stating that the interests of children and young people are paramount in all considerations of welfare and safeguarding.

• In 1990 The United Nations Convention published 'The Rights of the Child', which has 54 articles covering every aspect of a child's life, affirming that every child has rights too.

The above can obviously encourage parents to fight for their child's rights when necessary. If only they had been published for me to quote to Rachel's teachers when fighting for her!

Parents often feel inhibited about 'making a fuss' when arguing against professionals or fighting authorities but I advise anyone concerned that their child's problem is being ignored is, 'Don't be afraid to ask for a second opinion.' Both you and your child have rights! Doctors, Health Visitors and Teachers can all refer them to various agencies including Speech and Language Therapists and Educational Psychologists to investigate whether or not a child has any difficulties in learning.

Useful Names and Numbers

Afasic: a parent-led organisation that helps children and young people with speech and language impairments and their families.

Address: 15 Old Ford Road, St Margaret's House, London E2 9PJ

Helpline: 0300 666 9410

Telephone: 020 7490 9410

I CAN's mission is that no child should be left out or left behind because of a difficulty speaking or understanding.

Address: 31 Angel Gate (Gate 5), Goswell Road, London EC1V 2PT

Email: info@ican.org.uk

Printed in Poland
by Amazon Fulfillment
Poland Sp. z o.o., Wrocław

54497894R00058